D0769159

Nuclear Weapons

Other titles in the Issues in Focus *series:*

Nuclear Weapons

More Countries, More Threats

Tom Streissguth

Enslow Publishers, Inc.

40 Industrial Road	PO Box 38
Box 398	Aldershot
Berkeley Heights, NJ 07922	Hants GU12 6BP
USA	UK

http://www.enslow.com

Library of Congress Cataloging-in-Publication Data

Streissguth, Thomas, 1958–
     Nuclear weapons : more countries, more threats / Tom Streissguth.
        p. cm. — (Issues in focus)
     Includes bibliographical references (p. 99) and index.
     Summary: Traces the development of nuclear weapons, explains
the different types, indicates the key countries in the nuclear arms
race, and describes efforts taken to cease proliferation of such
weapons.
     ISBN 0-7660-1248-4 (hardcover)
     1. Nuclear weapons—Juvenile literature. 2. Nuclear arms
control—Juvenile literature. [1. Nuclear weapons. 2. Nuclear arms
control.] I. Title. II. Issues in focus (Hillside, N.J.)
     U264 .S78   2000
     355.8'25119—dc21

                                        99-050599

Printed in the United States of America

10 9 8 7 6 5 4 3 2 1

To Our Readers: All Internet addresses in this book were active and
appropriate when we went to press. Any comments or suggestions can
be sent by e-mail to Comments@enslow.com or to the address on the
back cover.

Illustration Credits: AP/Wide World Photos, p. 94; Library of
Congress, pp. 11, 13, 15, 29, 39, 53, 65, 79; National
Archives, pp. 9, 18, 27, 37, 47, 49, 75, 88.

Cover Illustration: National Archives, Department of Energy.

Contents

1

A Cloud Over the World

A flash of light appears in the sky. A powerful wave of energy damages computers, electronic equipment, and telephone lines. Dust from the blinding fireball rises into the atmosphere, forming an enormous, mushroom-shaped cloud. With the energy of 20 million tons of TNT, a 20-megaton nuclear weapon has just exploded over a point called "ground zero."

A thermal pulse, containing blinding light and great heat, spreads over the countryside. The pulse burns and kills plants, animals, and humans. A blast wave disintegrates every building within ten miles of ground zero. The mushroom cloud draws soil up, and the soil absorbs a deadly energy known as radiation. Driven by the wind, the cloud of radioactive dust rains over cities hundreds of miles away. The cloud contaminates everything it touches.

The explosion transforms the land into a desert. No crops or vegetation will grow here for a long time. Thousands of people have died. For many years afterward, thousands more will starve to death, develop cancer, or die from radiation sickness.

For now, a 20-megaton nuclear attack is imaginary. It might never happen. It could happen tomorrow or next week. Thousands of weapons of mass destruction exist. A number of countries are building them or buying them. Terrorist groups may be planning to steal them. Political and military leaders are prepared to use them.

Discovering Nuclear Energy

Nuclear weapons were made possible by the work and the discoveries of many scientists. It all began in 1896, when the French scientist Antoine Henri Becquerel found that the chemical element uranium gives off energy. As Becquerel imagined it, the energy, called radiation, came in the form of invisible rays. Substances that give off radiation are said to be radioactive.

Marie Curie, a Polish scientist living in Paris, investigated uranium as well as radium, a radioactive element that she discovered while working with her husband, Pierre Curie. During World War I

A posed photograph taken in 1918 by Major Everts Tracey of the United States Army Corps of Engineers, intended to show the effects of phosgene gas on front-line troops. For the first time, United States soldiers had to prepare for chemical weapons on the battlefield.

(1914–1918), Marie Curie brought instruments that detected radiation to the battlefields in northern France.

At this time, and for the first time in history, contending armies were using poison gas, manufactured in the factories of Germany, France, and Great Britain. Some poison gases, such as cyanide gas, were deadly. Some injured enemy soldiers by causing watering eyes, uncontrollable sneezing, blistering of the skin, or vomiting. The gases could also stop the lungs from working and kill by suffocation.

Other new weapons were being used in World War I. Airplanes and dirigibles (helium-filled airships) dropped bombs from the sky. Armored tanks rumbled across the battlefield, and submarines attacked while hiding under the surface of the sea. To bomb Paris, the capital of France, the Germans built a supergun known as the Paris Gun. The Paris Gun could throw an artillery shell about eighty miles. German gunners fired nearly three hundred rounds from this weapon in the spring and summer of 1918. The shells destroyed buildings and killed hundreds of civilians.[1] Paris was not a military target, however. The Paris Gun was a weapon designed to spread terror. Germany was losing World War I and wanted to scare the French leaders into asking for peace.

The terrible new weapons used in World War I frightened many political leaders. After the war, more than forty nations joined the League of Nations. This organization was supposed to help the world avoid another Great War, as the 1914–1918 conflict was then known. The members of the League signed the Geneva Protocol in 1925. This agreement banned the use of chemical weapons in warfare. At this time, the members of the League did not realize that even more destructive weapons would be available in the future.

Splitting the Atom

Scientists investigating radiation realized that this new form of energy might provide benefits in the future. They also understood that it carried dangers.

In this World War I print, intended for use with a stereoscopic (3-D) viewer, a United States soldier demonstrates how to use gas masks.

In high enough doses, radiation changes the chemical makeup of human cells, destroying them or changing them into cancer cells. Many scientists handling radium, a radioactive element, had been poisoned—including Marie Curie herself. Workers who painted radium on watches to make them glow had also gotten sick. Some developed cancer and died.

During the war, English scientist Ernest Rutherford also studied radiation and atoms, which he believed were the smallest parts of matter. During his experiments, he found that radiation was made of high-energy particles. There were two different kinds of such particles: alpha and beta.

Rutherford discovered that atoms have a nucleus, or center. In 1919, he tried an experiment. He bombarded the nuclei of nitrogen atoms with alpha particles. The nuclei changed, transforming the nitrogen into oxygen. Using radiation, he had changed one element into another.

In 1932, British scientist James Chadwick discovered the neutron, an atomic particle that lies inside the nucleus. In the next year, Hungarian scientist Leo Szilard thought of starting a chain reaction inside the atomic nucleus as a way of making a bomb. Szilard's idea took further shape in 1938, when the German scientists Otto Hahn and Fritz Strassman tried bombarding uranium with a stream of neutrons. This caused the atoms of uranium to fission, or split apart. The fissioning of the atoms also released energy.

Austrian physicist Lise Meitner and her nephew, physicist Otto Frisch, realized that uranium was the easiest of all elements to fission, because the arrangement of neutrons inside the uranium atom was less stable than in any other natural element. They also saw that fissioning the uranium atom, if done correctly, could start a chain reaction and release an incredible amount of energy.

To accomplish this, a certain amount of uranium

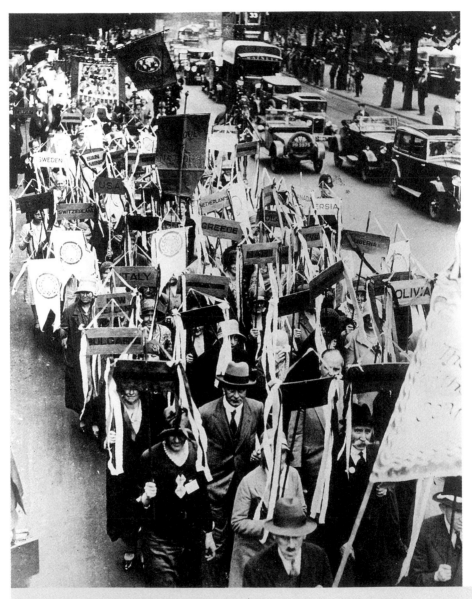

In a London parade for world disarmament during the 1920s, marchers carried signs with the name of each country in the League of Nations.

was needed—a "critical mass." If a chain reaction began inside a critical mass of uranium, an explosion would result. According to physicist Albert Einstein, the energy of this explosion could be expressed by the following mathematical equation:

$$E=mc^2$$
(E=energy, m=mass, c=the speed of light)

Through this and other equations, Einstein had proved that matter could be turned into energy— something that nobody had ever believed possible.

Einstein's famous equation showed that the energy of such an explosion would equal the mass of the atoms times the speed of light squared. Since the speed of light is 186,282 miles per second, a complete chain reaction would transform a single pound of uranium into a bomb with the force of 8,000 tons of TNT explosive.

The chain-reaction bomb would be thousands of times more powerful than any artillery shell. Because its force came from the energy stored inside the atom, it was called an atomic bomb.

World War II

Leo Szilard and Eugene Wigner, another Hungarian scientist, had both escaped from Nazi Germany during the 1930s. When they learned of the discoveries of Meitner and Frisch, they realized that Germany might build an atomic bomb. At this time, Germany was rebuilding its armed forces under the leadership of Adolf Hitler. Szilard and Wigner saw, as did many others, that Hitler might begin another Great War.

EINSTEIN TAKES UP THE SWORD

In this cartoon, physicist Albert Einstein sheds the wings of "Non-Resistant Pacifism" and takes up a sword labeled "Preparedness." Einstein left Germany in 1933 after the Nazis came to power. Previously known as a pacifist, he was calling on the world to unite against the oppression of Jews in his home country.

They wanted to warn the United States president, Franklin D. Roosevelt, about the bomb as soon as possible.

Szilard and Wigner asked Albert Einstein, who lived in the United States, to write a letter to the president.[2] Einstein was the most famous scientist in the world, and they believed that Roosevelt would pay attention to him. In October 1939, Roosevelt received a letter from Einstein, part of which read,

> I believe . . . that it is my duty to bring to your attention the following facts . . . it may become possible to set up nuclear chain reactions in a large mass of uranium, by which vast amounts of power and large quantities of new radium-like elements would be generated. . . . This new phenomenon would also lead to the construction of bombs and it is conceivable—though much less certain—that extremely powerful bombs of a new type may thus be constructed.[3]

By this time, Germany had already invaded Poland, and another world war had begun. While atomic research continued in the United States, British and Canadian scientists were also working toward the creation of an atomic bomb. Fearing the discovery of their atomic secrets by spies, the British gave their program the deceptive code name "Tube Alloys." The British government was determined to keep Tube Alloys separate and secret. British leaders did not want the United States to be the only country in the world with atomic weapons.[4]

In the fall of 1941, Roosevelt ordered an all-out effort to build the atomic bomb. The government gathered a group of scientists together and gave them their assignment: build a working atomic bomb, and quickly. A headquarters office began operating in Manhattan with the code name "Manhattan Project." Major General Leslie Groves was appointed its leader. Groves named J. Robert Oppenheimer as the Manhattan Project's chief scientist.

On December 7, 1941, two days after the Manhattan Project began, Japan attacked the United States by bombing Pearl Harbor, Hawaii. On the next day, the United States joined World War II by declaring war on Japan and Germany.

Building the Bomb

The Manhattan Project actually was carried out in several places far from Manhattan. Small research laboratories operated in Chicago and in Berkeley, California. The main research center was built in Los Alamos, New Mexico. Los Alamos lay in a remote desert, where towns and people were scarce. There, thousands of scientists, engineers, and military personnel worked in secret to assemble the atomic bomb.

From their calculations and study of the atomic nucleus, the Manhattan Project scientists learned that only a certain kind of uranium would chain-react and cause an atomic explosion. This kind of uranium was called U–235. The number 235 comes from the total of 143 neutrons and 92 protons (another atomic particle) that lie inside the nucleus of U–235.

Natural uranium, however, is made up mostly of

The Roosevelt administration placed Major General Leslie R. Groves in charge of the Manhattan Project.

U–238, a uranium isotope that has 146 neutrons and 92 protons. Only 0.7 percent of natural uranium is made up of U–235. For this reason, the scientists had to separate the U–235 from the U–238. They had to make enriched uranium, which contained more than 80 percent U–235. The enriched uranium could then be placed inside a bomb.

In the meantime, war was raging in Europe, Africa, and Asia. Germany was building new, long-distance weapons. At Peenemünde, a base along the North Sea, German scientists prepared a ballistic missile known as the V–2. ("Ballistic" meant that the missile would be launched, reach a certain height and speed, and then fall back to earth under the force of gravity.) The V–2 carried a ton of high explosives and had a range of 200 miles. From various launch sites in the Netherlands, the German scientists fired several hundred V–2s toward Great Britain.[5] They targeted cities and civilians rather than military bases. Like the Paris Gun, the V–2 was designed to terrorize people. V–2 rockets could, and did, destroy entire city blocks and killed many British civilians.

There was no stopping the V–2, the world's first successful ballistic missile. Yet while the V–2 program succeeded, the Germans failed to carry out the atomic bomb program so feared by Leo Szilard, Eugene Wigner, and Albert Einstein. German leaders believed such a project would be too costly. They sought instead to manufacture a great armory of conventional weapons—ships, planes, tanks, and artillery pieces. Politicians and scientists in the

United States were not aware of this decision until after the end of the war.[6] Throughout the war, they believed they were in a race with Germany to build the first atomic bomb.

Building the Bomb

The United States spent billions of dollars to build the atomic bomb, which also came to be known as a nuclear weapon (from the force of reactions inside the atomic nucleus). The project brought about many important scientific innovations. The first nuclear reactor, at the University of Chicago, created a controlled chain reaction of fissioning uranium atoms. At Oak Ridge, Tennessee, natural uranium was enriched for use in a nuclear weapon. The Hanford Engineer Work Plant in Richland, Washington, produced a manmade element called plutonium. Scientists had calculated that plutonium would make even better nuclear weapons material than enriched uranium.

The leaders of the Allied countries knew that nuclear weapons would be important in the future. To avoid any misunderstanding, they discussed the problem of how and when to use them. In August 1943, Prime Minister Winston Churchill of Great Britain and U.S. President Franklin D. Roosevelt signed the Quebec Agreement. This was the first nuclear treaty in history.

In the Quebec Agreement, the two leaders promised not to use nuclear weapons against each other. They also promised that neither would use them against a third country without an agreement from the other. The Quebec Agreement created a Combined Policy Committee. The Committee had Canadian, U.S., and British members. They would see that each country obeyed the agreement and that all would consent to any use of nuclear weapons.

Back at Los Alamos

Meanwhile, at the laboratories at Los Alamos, the scientists of the Manhattan Project were designing two different nuclear weapons. One of their designs was known as a uranium gun. Using a modified naval gun, one mass of U–235 would be fired at another. The impact would cause the U–235 to begin chain-reacting. The second design came in the form of a large sphere. Charges placed around the sphere exploded inward, creating a powerful implosion. The implosion compressed a smaller sphere of plutonium, starting a nuclear chain reaction.

In May 1945, an Interim Committee had been formed to decide how to proceed with a nuclear attack. The leader of the committee was Secretary of War Henry Stimson. On May 31, the committee considered using one bomb as a warning. But the members quickly decided against it. According to the minutes of the meeting:

> Secretary [Stimson] expressed the conclusion . . . that we could not give the Japanese any warning . . . but that we should seek to make a profound psychological impression on as many inhabitants as possible. At the suggestion of Dr. Conant, the Secretary agreed that the most desirable target would be a vital war plant employing a large

number of workers and closely surrounded by
workers' houses.[7]

In the meantime, a target committee under
General Groves had drawn up a list of four possible
target cities in Japan: Kyoto, Hiroshima, Kokura, and
Niigata. These cities would not be bombed or
attacked in any way until the nuclear weapons were
ready.

Soon after this decision, Stimson ordered Kyoto
taken off the list. Kyoto is an ancient religious and
cultural center of Japan. In his biography of Stimson,
Godfrey Hodgson put forth this possible reason for
his decision:

> What persuaded the secretary to dig in to spare
> Kyoto was the chance visit of a cousin, Henry
> Loomis, who had dined with the Stimsons . . . only
> a few months before. Young Loomis had taken
> courses at Harvard on Chinese and Japanese
> history and culture. . . . It was his innocent
> enthusiasm for the glories of Japanese art in
> general and of Kyoto in particular that stuck in the
> Secretary of War's mind.[8]

Secretary of War Stimson also may have feared
that bombing Kyoto would make Japan a permanent,
bitter enemy of the United States. To replace Kyoto,
the target committee chose the city of Nagasaki.

President Truman's Decisions

In May 1945, Germany had surrendered, ending
World War II in Europe. But the war was still on
against Japan in the Pacific Ocean. The United States
defeated Japanese forces in hard-fought, bloody

campaigns on the islands of Iwo Jima and Okinawa. The U.S. Navy, Marines, and Army prepared for an invasion of the "home islands" of Japan itself.

The plans called for the army and the marines, along with British and Australian forces, to land on Kyushu, the southernmost island of Japan, and then on Honshu, the largest island. They would then fight their way north to Tokyo, the Japanese capital.

Military planners told President Harry S. Truman that the invasion of Japan would probably cost thousands of lives. Fierce firebombing of Japan had not yet brought a surrender, and the Japanese military were prepared to defend the home islands. According to General George C. Marshall,

> We had one hundred thousand people killed in Tokyo in one night of bombs, and it had seemingly no effect whatsoever. It destroyed the Japanese cities, yes, but their morale was affected, so far as we could tell, not at all. So it seemed quite necessary, if we could, to shock them into action. . . . We had to end the war; we had to save American lives.[9]

President Truman agreed. He believed the Japanese leaders would not surrender unless they faced certain and total destruction. Yet he decided to give the Japanese an ultimatum before dropping the bomb. On July 25, he wrote in his diary,

> Even if the Japs are savages, ruthless, merciless, and fanatic, we as the leader of the world for the common welfare cannot drop this terrible bomb on the old capital [Kyoto] or the new [Tokyo]. . . . The target will be a purely military one and we will

issue a warning statement asking for Japs to surrender and save lives.[10]

Many of the scientists who had helped to create the bomb did not want the United States to use this weapon against civilians. Leo Szilard, who worked at Los Alamos, wrote a petition to J. Robert Oppenheimer demanding that the bomb not be used. On June 12, scientists working in Chicago sent a report to the secretary of war. The Franck Report supported a demonstration of the bomb in an uninhabited area. In part, the report said,

> If the United States were to be the first to release this new means of indiscriminate destruction upon mankind, she would sacrifice public support throughout the world. . . . Russia, and even allied countries which bear less mistrust of our ways and intentions, as well as neutral countries may be deeply shocked.[11]

The Franck Report also argued that if the bomb were used against Japan, it would start an international arms race after the war. If there were an arms race, it would be best to delay it as long as possible, and not use the bomb immediately, in order to give the United States a head start.

Testing the Atomic Bomb

Despite the petitions and reports, plans for using the new weapon raced ahead. On July 4, 1945, the Combined Policy Committee met secretly in Washington, D.C. The members approved the use of a nuclear weapon against Japan.

At 5:45 A.M. on July 16, 1945, in the desert near

Alamogordo, New Mexico, the scientists of the Manhattan Project set off the world's first nuclear explosion. The bomb sent up an enormous, mushroom-shaped cloud of dust and smoke. A witness named I. I. Rabi watched the explosion. Later, he described what he saw:

> Suddenly there was an enormous flash of light, the brightest light I have ever seen or that I think anyone has ever seen. It blasted; it pounced; it bored its way right through you. It was a vision which was seen with more than the eye. . . . Finally it was over . . . and we looked toward the place where the bomb had been; there was an enormous ball of fire which grew and grew and it rolled as it grew; it went up into the air; in yellow flashes and into scarlet and green. It looked menacing. It seemed to come toward one.[12]

Meanwhile, two bombs were sent to the Pacific island of Tinian. On Tinian, crews prepared B–29 Superfortress bomber planes to carry and drop the weapons. Members of the 509th Composite Group, under the command of Colonel Paul Tibbets, trained to fly the bombing runs to Japan.

General Groves and other officials had presented their plans for the bombing of Japan to President Truman. The president could have stopped the bombing or ordered it carried out as a warning. Instead, he decided to allow the bombing of target cities to proceed as planned. On July 25, General Thomas Handy, the Chief of Staff of the United States Army, gave the official order to General Carl Spaatz of the U.S. Army Strategic Air Force to drop the bomb: "The 509th

Composite Group, 20th Air Force, will deliver its special bomb as soon as weather will permit visual bombing after about 3 August 1945 on one of the targets . . ."[13]

On August 6, a B–29 bomber named *Enola Gay* took off for Hiroshima, Japan. At 9:15 A.M., at an elevation of 31,600 feet, the *Enola Gay* released its weapon, nicknamed Little Boy. The bomb exploded about 1,000 feet above the ground. The explosion destroyed four square miles of the city and killed more than 60,000 people.

John Hersey's book *Hiroshima* gives this eyewitness account of a Hiroshima civilian:

> Mr. Tanimoto saw an astonishing panorama . . . as much of Hiroshima as he could see through the clouded air was giving off a thick, dreadful miasma [vaporous fog]. Clumps of smoke, near and far, had begun to push up through the general dust. . . . Houses nearby were burning, and when huge drops of water the size of marbles began to fall, he half thought that they must be coming from the hoses of firemen fighting the blazes. (They were actually drops of condensed moisture falling from the turbulent tower of dust heat, and fission fragments that had already risen miles into the sky above Hiroshima).[14]

The survivors of Hiroshima remembered a blinding flash of light and then a powerful shock wave that destroyed buildings and bridges. Extreme heat vaporized people directly underneath the bomb at ground zero and burned many others caught outside. Fires ran out of control throughout the city for several hours. Thousands of people struggled to get

The Little Boy atomic bomb used a "uranium gun" to release a bomb that destroyed four square miles of the city of Hiroshima.

to wells or to a river for water, while many others hurried away from the center to escape the burning city.

Soon after the explosion, radioactive material began falling out of the sky over Hiroshima. This black rain caused radiation contamination in everything it touched: skin, clothing, water, food. Radiation from the bomb also poisoned the surrounding soil, buildings, and streets. In the days and weeks after the bombing, thousands of people died of radiation sickness. Typical symptoms included hair loss, bleeding gums, skin lesions, nausea, and diarrhea.

Those who survived the bombing are known to the Japanese as *hibakusha*.[15] They suffered burn scars, anemia, and cataracts. Children whose mothers were exposed to radiation from the bomb were mentally handicapped and physically deformed. *Hibakusha* also developed leukemia, a blood cancer, and several other cancers at a much higher rate than normal from the radiation they absorbed during the bombing.

Soon after the bombing, on August 6, President Truman issued a statement describing the bombing of Hiroshima and making another threat against Japan:

> Sixteen hours ago an American airplane dropped one atomic bomb on Hiroshima, an important Japanese Army base. That bomb had more power than 20,000 tons of TNT. . . .
>
> The Japanese began the war from the air at Pearl Harbor. They have been repaid many fold. . . . If they do not now accept our terms they may

expect a rain of ruin from the air, the like of which has never been seen on earth. Behind this air attack will follow sea and land forces in such numbers and power as they have not yet seen.[16]

On August 9, another nuclear bomb was dropped on Japan. This bomb, called Fat Man, exploded over the city of Nagasaki. It killed 36,000 people and destroyed another city. As described by a Japanese writer named Takashi Nagai in his book *The Bells of*

An aerial view of Nagasaki, Japan, reveals the destruction caused by the Fat Man atomic bomb, which was dropped on August 9, 1945.

Nagasaki, a farmer named Chimoto-san witnessed the explosion:

> Suddenly there was a blinding flash of light; an awful brightness but no noise. . . . In the area above the church he [Chimoto-san] saw an enormous column of white smoke float upward, swelling rapidly as it rose. But what struck terror into his heart was the huge blast of air like a hurricane that rushed toward him. Houses and trees and everything else collapsed before it. They fell to the ground; they were smashed to pieces; the debris was blown this way and that.
>
> Then a deafening noise struck his ears and he was thrown into the air and hurled five meters against a brick wall. Finally he opened his eyes and looked around. The trees were torn from their roots. There were no branches, no leaves, no grass. Everything had vanished.[17]

2

The Cold War

By mid–August 1945, the scientists at Los Alamos had built another plutonium bomb. The next target on the bombing list was the city of Kokura. But President Truman, in the meantime, had decided to stop the bombing. In a letter to Senator Richard Russell, who was demanding further nuclear attacks, Truman wrote:

> I know that Japan is a terribly cruel and uncivilized nation in warfare but I can't bring myself to believe that, because they are beasts, we should ourselves act in that same manner. . . . My object is to save as many American lives as possible but I also have a human feeling for the women and children of Japan.[1]

31

Historians, politicians, and military leaders have all questioned President Truman's decision to drop atomic bombs on Hiroshima and Nagasaki. Former President Dwight D. Eisenhower, the supreme commander of the Allied Expeditionary Force in Europe during World War II, later wrote:

> Japan was already defeated and . . . dropping the bomb was completely unnecessary. . . . I thought that our country should avoid shocking world opinion by the use of a weapon whose employment was, I thought, no longer mandatory as a measure to save American lives. It was my belief that Japan was, at that very moment, seeking some way to surrender.[2]

Japan did surrender a few days after the attack on Nagasaki, and World War II ended. But the bombing of Hiroshima and Nagasaki began a new era. The world now had to prepare for a nuclear arms race and a nuclear war.

The United States did not keep its nuclear secrets for long. During the war, a group of spies stole the plans for the implosion bomb from Los Alamos. The spies sent the plans to the Soviet Union, where a nuclear research program was already under way. By the end of the war, Soviet scientists were prepared to build an exact copy of the Fat Man bomb.

The Cold War

Writers had once called World War I "the war to end all wars." They were wrong. World War II turned out to be an even bigger and more destructive war. During World War II, millions of people died and many parts of Europe, Africa, and Asia were destroyed. For the first time, weapons of mass destruction were used.

Before the war ended, the United Nations (UN) was established. The UN would be a new, improved version of the League of Nations, which was formed after World War I as an international peace-keeping organization. (The United States had never joined the League.) The UN would allow people from every nation of the world to meet in one place to voice their differences. The UN would try to stop disputes before they turned into wars.

With its nuclear attack on Japan, the United States had changed warfare forever. Many people believed that the bomb made planes, tanks, and ships obsolete. Future wars would be fought with nuclear weapons. If World War III should break out, such weapons might bring the end of human civilization. In an article written for *Harper's* magazine in 1947, former Secretary of War Henry Stimson wrote,

> War in the twentieth century has grown steadily more barbarous, more destructive, more debased in all its aspects. Now with the release of atomic energy, man's ability to destroy himself is very nearly complete. The bombs dropped on Hiroshima and Nagasaki ended a war. They also made it wholly clear that we must never have another war.[3]

The possibility of global destruction did not stop political conflicts. During World War II, the Soviet Union and the United States were allies. But they also had completely different forms of government and different economic systems. The Communist

Soviet Union sought to make new allies all over the world, as did the United States, a capitalist nation. (Communist systems believe in economic development and control by the state, while capitalist governments believe in private enterprise by individuals.)

Because the countries were not directly fighting each other, this rivalry was called the Cold War. Both sides prepared for a real war in Europe. On the European continent, countries allied with the Soviet Union directly bordered countries allied with the United States.

President Truman wanted the United States to remain the world's only nuclear power. But Truman and Secretary of War Henry Stimson did not yet realize that the Soviet Union was already building its own weapons of mass destruction.

The Baruch Plan

After World War II ended, the U.S. Congress created the Atomic Energy Commission (AEC). The commissioners of the AEC would control the use of nuclear energy for peaceful and military purposes in the United States. They would control the building of nuclear reactors as well as nuclear weapons.

President Truman also proposed an international agency to control nuclear weapons. He asked Bernard Baruch, a wealthy businessman who also acted as an unofficial presidential adviser, to create a plan for the agency. Baruch's plan would set the rules for the

International Atomic Energy Commission, a part of the United Nations.

Baruch believed that a new international law should ban all nuclear weapons. No new weapons should be invented or built, and there should be very strict rules on the use of nuclear energy. An international agency would carry out inspections. Nations found to be violating the rules would be punished. When the nations of the world agreed to his plan, the United States would destroy its own nuclear weapons and stop making new ones.

In his speech to the United Nations introducing the plan, Baruch declared,

> We are here to make a choice between the quick and the dead. That is our business. Behind the black portent of the new atomic age lies a hope which, seized upon with faith, can work our salvation. If we fail, then we have damned every man to be the slave of Fear. Let us not deceive ourselves: We must elect World Peace or World Destruction.[4]

The leaders of the Soviet Union rejected the Baruch Plan. They believed it gave the United States an unfair advantage, as it would not allow their country to catch up with the nuclear program in the United States. The Soviet leaders offered a different plan, in which the world's countries would destroy all of their nuclear weapons within three months. According to this plan, there would be no inspections to make sure the plan was followed.

President Truman would not agree to the Soviet plan. He believed that the Soviet Union would never be able to build a nuclear bomb. He was sure that the United States would remain the world's only nuclear power.[5]

Baruch presented his plan to the United Nations on June 14, 1946. A majority of the members of the United Nations voted against the plan. A nuclear arms race was soon under way.

Explosions in the Pacific

The United States continued building and testing nuclear weapons. In the summer of 1946, an entire fleet of ships—to be used *only* for target practice—sailed to the Bikini Atoll, a string of islands in the Pacific Ocean. For the tests, code-named Operation Crossroads, the navy moved people living on the Bikini Atoll out of their homes. On July 1, the tests began. Two nuclear weapons were set off on the atoll. One exploded underwater; the other was dropped from an airplane. The bombs destroyed or damaged many of the target ships. A cloud of radiation settled on the atoll.

The Bikini Atoll tests made banner headlines all over the world. According to historian Jonathan Weisgall,

> The media attention given the tests was phenomenal. Nearly 2.5 million words and 400 photographs were transmitted by radio from Bikini to newspapers and magazines, together with 615 radio broadcasts. . . . in the days immediately following each test, more than 20 percent of front-page U.S. newspaper articles were devoted to Operation Crossroads.[6]

The testing of nuclear weapons at the Bikini Atoll in 1946 brought a strong protest from the Soviet Union, whose leaders accused the United States of sabotaging the first efforts at nuclear arms control.

The Bikini Atoll tests angered the Soviet Union and many other countries. They accused the United States of working against arms control. An article in *Pravda*, the official Soviet newspaper, complained that

> if the atomic bomb at Bikini did not explode anything wonderful, [it did] explode something more important than a couple of out-of-date warships; it fundamentally undermined the belief in the seriousness of American talk about atomic disarmament.[7]

Building a Nuclear Stockpile

More atomic tests took place. In April and May of 1948, nuclear weapons were exploded at Eniwetok Atoll in the Marshall Islands. The May 1 explosion had a yield of forty-nine kilotons, meaning it had the force of 49,000 tons of TNT. This yield was almost four times the size of the Hiroshima bomb. A new design made these weapons much more powerful than those used on Japan.

Military leaders in the United States were drawing up plans for fighting a nuclear war. This war plan called for the United States to drop fifty bombs on twenty different Soviet cities. United States officials believed this plan would be the only way to stop a Soviet attack on Western Europe.

Civilians in the United States also prepared themselves for a nuclear war. Many cities and small towns built air-raid shelters, where people were supposed to gather in case of nuclear attack. Some families built small underground bomb shelters in their backyards and stocked these shelters with food and water. School principals had their students go through air-raid drills, just in case. The students also watched instructional films that showed them what to do in case of a nuclear explosion. In one pamphlet, citizens were advised, "If you are inside, dive under or behind the nearest desk, table, sofa or other piece of sturdy furniture. Try to get in a shadow; it will help shade you from the heat. Lie curled on your side with your hands over the back of your neck, knees tucked against your chest."[8]

For her first weekly forum television broadcast, on February 11, 1950, Eleanor Roosevelt, the widow of President Franklin Roosevelt, chose for her topic, "What to Do About the Hydrogen Bomb." David Lilienthal, chairman of the Atomic Energy Commission (center), and J. Robert Oppenheimer (right) were among her guests.

After World War II, as millions of soldiers left the army, the United States cut its defense budget. Although the Soviet Union also demobilized millions of soldiers, it began strengthening its forces again in 1947.[9] The Soviets saw their conventional forces— soldiers, tanks, planes, and ships—as an important balance to U.S. atomic weapons.

Near Misses in Europe

In central Europe, Germany was now on the front line of the Cold War between the Soviet Union and the United States. At the end of the war, Germany was divided into two countries. The zones occupied by the United States, Great Britain, and France became West Germany. The Soviet zone of occupation became East Germany. The German capital, Berlin, was divided into East Berlin, occupied by the Soviets, and West Berlin, occupied by the United States, Great Britain, and France.

A confrontation took place over Berlin on June 24, 1948, when the Soviet Union closed all rail traffic to West Berlin. The people of West Berlin could not get any food or medicine from the outside. The blockade was meant to force this zone to surrender to Soviet control.

On July 1, the United States Air Force, as well as British and French aircraft, began an airlift of supplies to West Berlin. Air force planes flew day and night into a West Berlin airport. The airlift continued through the summer and fall of 1948. Many people feared another war if one of the airlift planes were shot down.

During the airlift, Winston Churchill made a suggestion to a United States ambassador, Lewis Douglas. Churchill thought that the United States should threaten atomic bombing if the Soviets did not stop the blockade of West Berlin. Douglas reported to President Truman that "He [Churchill] believes that now is the time, promptly, to tell the Soviet[s] that if they do not retire from Berlin and abandon Eastern Germany, withdrawing to the Polish frontier, we will raze their cities."[10]

General Curtis LeMay, the leader of the Strategic

Air Command, was also preparing to fight. He made a plan to bomb the Soviet Union and send armies across eastern Germany. The armies would force open a supply route from western Germany to West Berlin. If the Soviets kept fighting, the United States would use its nuclear weapons.

President Truman decided not to use LeMay's plan. He was determined not to start a nuclear war. Truman believed that nuclear weapons were most useful as terror weapons, to be used against civilian targets. Against military targets, conventional bombs could be just as destructive, if enough of them were used. Conventional bombs had another advantage: They did not spread radiation, which could poison friendly troops as well as the enemy.

The Berlin airlift ended in January 1949. The Soviet Union backed down and allowed supply trains to again reach West Berlin. Three months later, the United States and eleven other nations agreed to form a new military alliance. The alliance was called the North Atlantic Treaty Organization (NATO). Each nation agreed to help the others in case of a Soviet attack.

Going Nuclear

After World War II, the Soviet leader Josef Stalin ordered scientists in his country to build nuclear weapons. The scientists already had a good head start. A spy named Harry Gold had been given the plans for the Fat Man plutonium bomb by Klaus Fuchs and David Greenglass, laboratory workers at

Los Alamos. Gold passed on the plans to the Soviet Union.[11] Using the plans, Soviet scientists assembled their first nuclear weapon at Chelyabinsk, a site east of the Ural Mountains in Siberia. On August 29, 1949, the bomb was tested at Semipalatinsk, in the Soviet republic of Kazakhstan. The explosion had a yield of twenty kilotons, about five kilotons greater than the power of the Hiroshima bomb.

The Soviet test was top secret. But then, on September 3, a U.S. reconnaissance plane detected radioactivity near the Pacific coast of the Soviet Union. The radiation cloud came from the west and was drifting eastward. It passed over Canada, the northern United States, the Atlantic Ocean, and finally northern Europe.

Such a cloud could only have been created by the explosion of a nuclear weapon. When he heard about the test, President Truman realized he had been wrong. The United States could not keep its nuclear secrets.

The Cold War had grown more dangerous. Both superpowers were now building and testing nuclear weapons. If a war began, either side might try to gain a quick advantage by using these weapons. There would not be much time to make the decision. A conventional war might go nuclear in a matter of hours or minutes.

The Atomic Age

Germany was not the only nation to suffer division after World War II. After the surrender of Japan, the Asian nation of Korea was also divided. Soviet troops occupied northern Korea, while the United States occupied the south. The country had separate northern and southern governments.

In 1948, the nations of South Korea and North Korea were established. The Soviet Union and the United States then withdrew their troops. On June 25, 1950, North Korea invaded South Korea. The General Assembly of the United Nations voted to intervene. The United States sent troops to fight the invasion of South Korea.

The Cold War had reached a new, more dangerous stage. In November 1950, forces from Communist China joined the North Koreans. Communist China and the United States were now fighting each other. The concern was that the fighting might spread outside Korea, and it threatened to go nuclear if the Soviet Union entered the war.

As the Korean War dragged on through early 1953, neither side gained an advantage. The stalemate frustrated U.S. military leaders. General Douglas MacArthur asked the president to consider using nuclear weapons to prevent Chinese or Soviet troops from invading and conquering South Korea.

Truman decided not to use nuclear weapons in Korea. He feared that it would bring the Soviet Union directly into the war and touch off World War III. Truman knew that he would be blamed if the Korean War turned into a worldwide nuclear disaster. He also knew that a nuclear attack would anger Asian allies of the United States. It would have been the second nuclear attack by the United States on an Asian country.[1]

The Korean War ended with a cease-fire declared on July 27, 1953. Almost fifty years later, Korea remains a divided country. North Korean leaders still run a Communist system of government, while South Korea remains a close ally of the United States. North and South Korea have never signed a peace treaty, and North Korea still has a huge army ready to attack the south. The leaders of North Korea also are testing long-range missiles that are capable of carrying nuclear warheads as far as the Pacific Ocean and the western coast of North America.[2]

The Hydrogen Bomb

The first Soviet nuclear test in August 1949 surprised the United States. To meet the threat, the U.S. government came up with a new policy: build up its nuclear arsenal as quickly as possible. The arsenal must be so powerful that the Soviets would never dare to attack it. It must also discourage the Soviets from threatening United States allies around the world.

Lewis Strauss, the chairman of the Atomic Energy Commission, proposed another way to meet the threat: "We should now make an intensive effort to get ahead with the [new bomb]. By intensive effort, I am thinking of a commitment in talent and money comparable, if necessary, to that which produced the first atomic bomb. That is the way to stay ahead."[3]

Strauss was talking about a new weapon of mass destruction designed by a Los Alamos scientist named Edward Teller. An explosion of this bomb would set off a chain reaction among atoms of hydrogen. The resulting high temperatures would then combine, or fuse, atoms instead of splitting them, as in the atomic bomb.

The hydrogen bomb would be much more powerful than the bombs used against Hiroshima and Nagasaki. A single gram of hydrogen bomb material set off by nuclear fusion would create an explosion equal to 150 tons of TNT. This was eight times the force of the explosion created by chain-reacting U–235. The hydrogen bomb would again give the United States superiority in the arms race.

President Truman had given his approval to the project. But many of the scientists working on the hydrogen bomb were frightened by what they were creating. They considered one possibility: The bomb could ignite hydrogen in the atmosphere and cause the entire planet to explode. J. Robert Oppenheimer wrote of the hydrogen bomb:

> This thing appears to have caught the imagination both of the Congressional and the military people, as the answer to the problem posed by the Russian advance. . . . [To] become committed to it as the way to save the country and the peace appears to me full of dangers.[4]

Military leaders in the United States said it would be foolish not to have the hydrogen bomb. They believed the Soviets might be creating a similar bomb in their laboratories. President Truman saw the hydrogen bomb as a useful bargaining chip. He would simply let the Soviets know that the United States could use this awesome weapon, if necessary.

In October 1952, a team of scientists sailed to Eniwetok Atoll in the Pacific Ocean. There they prepared to set off the first working hydrogen bomb, nicknamed Mike. In the early morning hours of November 1, Mike exploded, causing a three-mile-wide fireball that reached a height of almost twenty miles. As radioactive mud and rain fell out of the sky, the explosion carved a crater 200 feet deep and a

During a nuclear test in 1952, soldiers clown around for the camera. Many troops were ordered to witness nuclear explosions near ground zero to test the effects of the new weapons on battlefield combatants.

mile wide in the atoll. The Mike bomb had a yield of 10.4 megatons, making it about 600 times bigger than the bomb that destroyed much of Hiroshima.

Proliferating Weapons

In the meantime, nuclear weapons were spreading beyond the two superpowers. In 1952, Great Britain tested its first nuclear weapon in the remote deserts of Australia. France and China were also preparing their own nuclear weapons programs.

In the United States, nuclear scientists were

inventing new ways of delivering the bombs. Instead of dropping them from airplanes, these new systems would use intercontinental ballistic missiles (ICBMs). The United States could fire ICBMs from launching pads inside the nation at the Soviet Union.

Scientists also designed a new missile, the Jupiter, by copying plans for the German V–2 from launching pads. Instead of high explosive, the Jupiter carried a 1.5-megaton nuclear warhead that could travel 1,700 miles. The United States would base Jupiter missiles in Italy and Turkey. From these places, the Jupiter missile could hit targets inside the Soviet Union.

The United States Navy designed new submarines to carry ballistic missiles. Using nuclear energy, the submarines could cruise underwater, undetected by radar, for months. They held smaller nuclear missiles nicknamed Polaris, which they could launch close to the Soviet coast.

Sputnik

In May 1955, the Soviet Union and its allies in Europe organized the Warsaw Pact. This military alliance was meant to balance the power of NATO, whose most powerful member was the United States.

Soviet scientists were hard at work as well. In August 1957, the Soviets announced that they had built an ICBM. On October 4, the Soviet Union launched the *Sputnik* satellite. The satellite was very small—only 22 inches in diameter—and weighed only 184 pounds. Traveling at five miles per second,

This basement fallout shelter, photographed in 1957, includes a fourteen-day supply of food and water as well as other equipment. Many families built such structures in the 1950s and 1960s to prepare for a nuclear war.

Sputnik passed over Europe, India, the Middle East, the Pacific Ocean, and the United States. One month later, *Sputnik II* was launched. This satellite was much larger, and it carried the first space traveler, a dog named Laika. The satellites were not yet considered safe for humans.

The *Sputnik* launches were a victory for the Soviet Union in the race to explore outer space. They also represented a victory in the arms race. The Soviets had used a missile to carry *Sputnik*. Such a missile could carry nuclear weapons as well as passengers and radio equipment. The *Sputnik* satellite itself was harmless, but to politicians and military leaders in the United States, its successful launch represented the most serious threat yet of the Cold War.

A Dangerous Incident

In the late 1950s, the United States had its own methods of spying on the Soviet Union. The air force was sending a jet-powered glider plane, the U–2, over Soviet territory to take photographs of the Soviet secret cities and their activities. The U–2 could fly as high as 70,000 feet.

On May 1, 1960, Francis Gary Powers took off in a U–2 spy plane. The plane's mission was to photograph the Soviet ICBM launch site at Tyuratam, where *Sputnik* had been launched. At 68,000 feet, a surface-to-air (SAM) missile hit the plane. Powers ejected and the plane crashed.

The United States Department of State claimed that the plane was an unarmed weather research plane, that the plane's oxygen had failed, and that the pilot had lost consciousness. By accident, the plane had drifted over the Soviet Union. Soviet Premier Nikita Khrushchev then revealed that the pilot had been captured. Film found on board the plane had been developed. The photographs showed Soviet weapons sites. President Eisenhower admitted to spying on the Soviet Union.

Khrushchev demanded an immediate end to spy flights. He withdrew an invitation for Eisenhower to visit the Soviet Union. The Soviet leader also canceled a summit (high-level) meeting scheduled to take place in Paris.

The Cuban Missile Crisis

By the early 1960s, the Soviet Union and the United States each had enough nuclear weapons to cause millions of deaths and widespread devastation. A nuclear war now threatened not just the destruction of cities, but entire nations. The world came very close to such a war in the fall of 1962, when the United States and the Soviet Union prepared to fight over the island nation of Cuba.

On January 1, 1959, Fidel Castro took control of Cuba, which lies ninety miles south of the state of Florida. Castro adopted the Communist system and drew close to the Soviet Union. The government of the United States saw Castro as a threat and wanted the Cuban leader removed from power.

On October 14, 1962, a U–2 spy plane discovered missile-launching sites as well as two medium-range ballistic missiles at San Cristobal, southwest of Havana, Cuba. These SS–4 missiles were one-megaton Soviet weapons with a range of 1,100 miles—meaning they could reach Washington, D.C. Cuba also had mobile launchers, which could be moved by train or truck.[5]

Castro had asked for the weapons to guard Cuba against the United States. The Soviet commanders had orders to use the weapons against any invasion. The decision to use these weapons was up to them.

They would not have to wait for permission from their superiors in the Soviet Union to start a nuclear war.

The United States discovered the missiles and missile sites in photographs taken by a high-flying reconnaissance plane. President John F. Kennedy demanded that the Soviet Union dismantle the sites and remove any missiles from Cuba. Kennedy told United States military leaders that he would invade Cuba if the Soviets did not agree to his terms. The United States Navy began a blockade of Cuba. Nineteen ships were spread out across the Atlantic Ocean. The ships had orders to stop any Soviet ships sailing to Cuba.

The Soviets decided to defy the blockade. In Washington, D.C., a Soviet commander, Lieutenant General Vladimir Dubovik, announced,

> I have fought in three wars already, and I am looking forward to fighting in the next. We Russians are ready to defend ourselves against any act of aggression, against ourselves or any of our allies. Our ships will sail through. And if it is decreed that those men must die, then they will obey their orders and stay on course, or be sunk.[6]

Several Soviet ships were boarded by U.S. Navy commanders. The U.S. Army moved antiaircraft batteries into southern Florida. The military prepared the final plans for invading Cuba.

But on Sunday, October 28, the Soviet leader, Nikita Khrushchev, agreed to remove the missile sites if the United States agreed not to invade Cuba. The

On October 24, 1962, President John F. Kennedy signed a presidential proclamation entitled "Interdiction of the Delivery of Offensive Weapons to Cuba." Having discovered Soviet medium-range missiles just ninety miles from the United States, Kennedy confronted Soviet Premier Nikita Khrushchev and demanded that the missiles be removed. For a week, the two superpowers drew close to an all-out nuclear war.

United States also agreed to remove Jupiter missiles from their bases in northern Turkey.

Had Kennedy ordered the invasion of Cuba, Soviet forces on the island would have been outnumbered. To defend themselves, Soviet commanders in Cuba might have decided to launch their nuclear missiles against U.S. troops. United States military leaders then might have advised Kennedy to launch a nuclear attack against the Soviet Union. The result would have been an all-out nuclear war.

The Cuban Missile Crisis ended peacefully. Nevertheless, the United States and the Soviet Union had come to the brink of a nuclear war. If another crisis were to follow—in Berlin, Korea, or some other Cold War hot spot—the world would again face disaster.

Heads of state in both nations began thinking of ways to make a nuclear war less likely. In a speech, President Kennedy remarked, "It is therefore our intention to challenge the Soviet Union, not to an arms race, but to a peace race: to advance together step by step, stage by stage, until general and complete disarmament has actually been achieved."[7]

Effects of Nuclear War on People and the Environment

Despite the dangers of nuclear proliferation, testing of nuclear weapons by the United States, the Soviet Union, and other nations continued. France had set off its first nuclear explosion in 1960, in the North African colony of Algeria. The People's Republic of

China would become a nuclear power with a test at Lop Nor, in the province of Xingjiang, on October 16, 1964.

Meanwhile, scientists were learning more about the effects of nuclear war on humans. By studying the survivors of Hiroshima and Nagasaki, scientists learned that exposure to a nuclear explosion can cause a lifetime of sickness. Many years after the event, it can cause leukemia, cataracts, and sterility. Thousands of survivors in Hiroshima and Nagasaki suffered burn scars known as keloids, which take years to heal and in some cases are permanent. The bombings also caused deformities and mental handicaps among children whose pregnant mothers had been exposed to radiation.[8]

In May 1962, an article in the *New England Journal of Medicine* described in terrible detail the effects a 20-megaton explosion over Boston, Massachusetts, would have if a nuclear attack ever occurred. The fireball would raise temperatures to 20 million degrees Fahrenheit at ground zero. A firestorm would destroy everything—houses, buildings, trees, people, cars—within a thirty-mile radius. One million people would die within minutes, and more than one million would later die from their injuries. Radiation sickness would cause nausea, vomiting, diarrhea, convulsions, coma, and death. Radiation would also cause bone marrow to stop producing white blood cells in people who survived. With a lowered white-blood-cell count, they would suffer a series of harmful infections. Because radiation also reduces the number of platelets, which help to clot the blood, survivors would also suffer heavy internal bleeding.[9]

The testing of nuclear weapons was also beginning to affect the earth's environment. Nuclear explosions were raising levels of radiation in the air and soil around the world. The fallout brought high levels of strontium–90, a radioactive isotope. (Isotopes are different kinds of atoms of the same element; for example, the isotopes U–235 and U–238 are different varieties of uranium.) Strontium–90 contaminates plants through their leaves and roots. It also causes leukemia and other cancers in human beings. If nuclear testing continued, fallout of strontium–90 could begin to contaminate the world's food supply.

Fallout from nuclear testing in the 1960s and 1970s in the western United States also caused a rise in the level of the isotope iodine–131. In 1982, the National Cancer Institute estimated that this rise resulted in between 10,000 and 75,000 new cases of thyroid cancer. Radiation from the testing also found its way to cows' milk. Because milk was an important part of their diet, children living near the test sites were exposed to greater concentrations of radioactive isotopes than adults.[10]

As of June 1, 1998, a grand total of 2,051 nuclear tests had taken place on earth, 528 taking place in the earth's atmosphere.[11] In addition, radiation has been released from factories that produce weapons and bomb-grade uranium and plutonium. At the Hanford site in the Columbia River valley of Washington State, nuclear weapons production has been taking place for more than forty years, and the site is proving dangerous to nearby residents and livestock. Radiation has been released through routine emissions as well as sloppy management, wrote author Michael D'Antonio in *Atomic Harvest: Hanford and the Lethal Toll of America's Nuclear Arsenal:*

> . . . 177 steel waste tanks—some dating back to the Manhattan Project . . . were buried in the ground near various processing facilities. More than 60 million gallons of highly radioactive sludge had been deposited in these tanks over the years. Sixty-seven of them were known "leakers," and pools of radioactive liquid had descended beneath them toward the water table.[12]

Dangers of "Peaceful" Plutonium

In other ways, the use of nuclear energy, even for peaceful purposes, brings environmental as well as military dangers. By the 1990s, more civilian than military programs were using plutonium. Of the 1,200 tons of plutonium created since World War II, only 260 tons have been used in weapons. The rest has been used in nuclear reactors designed to generate electricity.[13]

Plutonium is one of the most toxic substances on earth. Tiny amounts of this radioactive element can cause cancer. If plutonium is accidentally released into the atmosphere, it can contaminate the air and soil in a large area for thousands of years.

Scientists have learned how to reprocess this civilian plutonium after it has been used to fuel nuclear reactors. After it has been reprocessed, the plutonium can then be used in a nuclear weapon. As more and more "peaceful" plutonium is created, the risks grow that a terrorist group will steal this dangerous bomb fuel, or that it will be sold to a country seeking to build its first nuclear weapon.

In the 1990s, the United States launched two satellites, named *Galileo* and *Cassini*, that were powered by plutonium-fueled nuclear reactors. In order to send the satellites to distant planets, flight engineers sent them skipping off the earth's atmosphere, where the earth's gravity worked like a slingshot to increase the satellites' speed. But many environmental and antinuclear groups protested these flybys. If an accident happens, and a nuclear-powered satellite comes crashing back to earth, released plutonium might create a global environmental disaster.

4

Making Treaties

In July 1963, the United States, the Soviet Union, and Great Britain signed the treaty banning nuclear weapons tests in the atmosphere, in outer space, and under water. The treaty was called the Limited Test Ban Treaty because testing would still be permitted underground. Scientists believed underground testing would do the least damage to soil, air, and water.

The U.S. Senate ratified the test ban treaty in September 1963 and the treaty entered into force in October. More treaties followed later in the 1960s. The countries of Latin America signed a treaty prohibiting nuclear weapons in 1967. This treaty made South and Central America—and the Caribbean region that included Cuba—the first zone on earth to be legally nuclear weapon–free. It did not stop wealthier Latin American countries, such as Brazil, from building parts that could some-day be used in nuclear weapons.

Despite the treaties, problems remained. Nuclear weapons were quickly proliferating outside of the world's two superpowers—the United States and the Soviet Union. In 1967, France set up its own nuclear force, called the *force de frappe* (Striking Force). This force included land-based missiles, submarines, and aircraft. According to historian Robert Cole, "Its [the *force de frappe*'s] function was as much diplomatic as military: having 'the bomb' guaranteed French membership in the 'nuclear club,' and that France would be consulted whenever there was an international crisis—which simply is one definition of a great power."[1]

In the same year, the French president, Charles de Gaulle, withdrew his country from NATO. French leaders declared they were not allied with either the United States or the Soviet Union. They would remain independent of the superpowers.

Other nonaligned countries in the world noticed. Any country could go its own way and build its own independent nuclear force. It could test these weapons on its own, build missile bases, and make itself a nuclear power.

The Non-proliferation Treaty

To counter the spread of nuclear weapons, a treaty called the Non-proliferation of Nuclear Weapons

Treaty was signed in 1968. The Non-proliferation Treaty (NPT) required all nations that signed it to keep records of their use of nuclear materials. The records would show the source and amount of plutonium and uranium used in nuclear reactors. These figures would be reported to the International Atomic Energy Agency (IAEA) in Vienna, Austria.

More than one hundred thirty countries have signed the NPT. In all of these nations, IAEA inspectors have the right to inspect nuclear facilities of any kind. They also may set up cameras to film the activities in nuclear facilities. But the NPT has not stopped the spread of nuclear technology. Several nuclear powers—including India and Pakistan—have not signed it. Other countries that have signed the NPT still buy and sell missiles and equipment they can use to build a nuclear military force. A black market in enriched uranium and plutonium allows these countries to obtain explosive material secretly.

New Weapons

While signing these agreements, the United States and the Soviet Union pressed ahead with their own nuclear research. The Soviet Union developed antiballistic missiles (ABMs). These weapons are designed to bring down enemy missiles in midflight. To meet this challenge, the United States invented a system known as Multiple Independently Targetable Reentry Vehicles, or MIRVs.

A MIRV system carries several nuclear warheads atop a single missile. In flight, the nose of the MIRV opens and the warheads fly to their separate targets. No single ABM or antiaircraft missile can destroy every warhead. Although the United States designed the MIRV system to make Soviet ABMs obsolete, the Soviet Union soon designed a MIRV system of its own.

By the end of the 1960s, both the Soviet Union and the United States had built up huge nuclear arsenals. The United States still feared an invasion of Western Europe by members of the Warsaw Pact, an organization that included most Eastern European nations. Because Warsaw Pact forces would outnumber NATO forces, the United States planned to respond to such an invasion with nuclear weapons.

Both sides believed they could avoid nuclear war, however. United States planners came up with a theory called Mutual Assured Destruction, or MAD. This theory was based on the idea that during a war both sides would target enemy cities and prepare to launch nuclear missiles. But neither side would actually start a nuclear war. Leaders on both sides knew such a war would mean the destruction of their own country. Many people believed that Mutual Assured Destruction would keep the world free of nuclear war.

The MAD theory uses the idea that nuclear weapons actually deter war. According to this theory, the fear of a nuclear reprisal will stop anyone from starting a fight with a nuclear power such as the Soviet Union or the United States. In this way, nuclear weapons serve to keep the peace. Some civilian and military strategists use the theory of deterrence to support the building of nuclear weapons.

The SALT Agreements

More treaty meetings began in November 1969 with the Strategic Arms Limitation Talks (SALT). The United States sought to make the arsenals of the two superpowers roughly equal. The United States also wanted to make sure that it could check that the Soviet Union was following any nuclear treaty the two nations signed.

The SALT talks continued for several years. Negotiators worked out limits on the number of land-launched and submarine-launched missiles each side could have. They also agreed on the number of submarines. The SALT treaty was signed in May 1972 by President Richard Nixon and Soviet Premier Leonid Brezhnev. At the same time, the two leaders signed a separate treaty on ABM systems. This treaty limited each nation to two ABM sites, with no more than one hundred missiles to be based at each site.

In 1973, SALT II negotiations began. The new treaty would set limits on all nuclear weapons systems. Eventually, it would begin to reduce arsenals. In November 1974, in the Soviet port city of Vladivostok, the two sides worked out a compromise. The treaty would allow each side to have 2,400 land-launched missiles, submarine-launched missiles, and long-range bombers. Each side could also have 1,320 MIRV warheads.[2] The treaty would do nothing to cut nuclear arsenals, however. Neither side had yet built that many weapons.

Argument over the treaty continued until June 1979. In that month, the two sides agreed to the final text of the SALT II agreement. On June 18, President Jimmy Carter and Premier Leonid Brezhnev signed the treaty in Vienna.

President Carter and SALT II would run into trouble at home, however. According to the United States Constitution, two thirds of the members of the United States Senate must approve any foreign treaty signed by the president. Many senators opposed the treaty. They accused President Carter of giving the Soviets an unfair advantage. After the Soviet Union invaded Afghanistan in December 1979, Carter criticized the Soviets. He also withdrew the SALT II treaty from consideration by the Senate.[3]

A New President and New Missiles

In 1980, Ronald Reagan became president. President Reagan criticized the SALT II agreement. He accused former President Carter of neglecting the nuclear arsenal of the United States. The Reagan administration set out to rebuild the arsenal.

The Soviet Union had placed intermediate-range missiles in Eastern Europe. Soviet commanders aimed the missiles, called SS–20s, at cities in Western Europe. Each of the SS–20s was capable of carrying three nuclear warheads. To match the SS–20s, the United States and NATO announced that ground-launched cruise missiles would be placed in Western

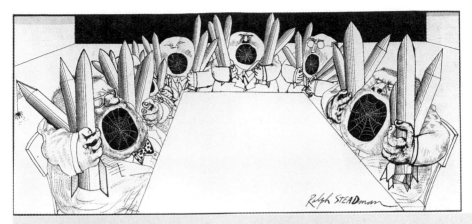

Cartoonist Ralph Steadman satirized world leaders and arms-control efforts during the SALT negotiations in 1971.

Europe. Pershing II ballistic missiles would also be based in Europe. The Pershing missiles, all nuclear-capable, were designed as battlefield weapons, to be used by competing armies during a war on the ground.

The Reagan administration believed the new missiles would help in future treaty talks with the Soviets. But many people in Europe did not want the missiles on their territory. They believed the missiles raised the chances for a nuclear war. Huge anti-nuclear parades took place, and Western European governments criticized the actions of NATO and the Warsaw Pact.

In July 1982, European opposition to the new missiles persuaded the Reagan administration to open new weapons talks. During these Intermediate-Range Nuclear Force (INF) talks, negotiators Paul Nitze of the United States and Yuli Kvitsinsky of the

Soviet Union met privately on a Swiss mountain.
They reached an agreement: the Soviets would cut
SS–20s by two thirds, to seventy-five. The United
States would deploy only three hundred nuclear warheads on its cruise missiles, which could themselves
be armed with either conventional (non-nuclear) or
nuclear devices. The U.S. government also agreed to
take all Pershing missiles out of service.[4]

Angered at Nitze's making the agreement without
his approval, President Reagan rejected it. Reagan
proposed that the United States and the Soviet Union
not deploy any intermediate-range missiles. The
Soviets turned down this zero-option idea. In
November 1983, NATO began the deployment of its
cruise missiles in Western Europe. The Soviet Union
withdrew from the INF talks. They also withdrew
from the Strategic Arms Reduction Treaty (START)
talks, which were designed to reduce the total
number of nuclear warheads on both sides.

The Reagan administration also began develop-
ment of a new defense system known as the Strategic
Defense Initiative, or Star Wars. In a speech given on
March 23, 1983, President Reagan introduced Star
Wars:

> Let me share with you a vision of the future which
> offers hope. It is that we embark on a program to
> counter the awesome Soviet missile threat with
> measures that are defensive . . . what if free
> people could live secure in the knowledge that
> their security did not rest upon the threat of
> instant U.S. retaliation to deter a Soviet attack,
> that we could intercept and destroy strategic

ballistic missiles before they reached our own soil or that of our allies?[5]

Star Wars would be a system of orbital satellites that would warn of a nuclear attack. The Star Wars system was also designed to stop a nuclear attack with defensive weapons based in space.

But to the Soviets, Star Wars seemed to pose the threat of nuclear attack on their territory from outer space. After Reagan introduced Star Wars, Soviet negotiators asked the United States to end Star Wars research as a condition of further cuts in their own arsenal.

While the negotiating continued, the world was reminded of the dangers of using nuclear energy. On April 24, 1986, a nuclear energy plant at Chernobyl, inside the Soviet Union, experienced a meltdown, an uncontrolled chain reaction that destroyed its reactor. The accident released a cloud of radiation into the air over the Soviet republics of Ukraine and Belarus, and over much of northern Europe. For thirty kilometers around Chernobyl, the soil was contaminated. Nearly three thousand villages in Belarus were also poisoned. Australia-born physician Helen Caldicott, a leading antinuclear writer, claimed the accident forced 90,000 evacuations, caused deformities in children born to mothers in the region, and placed 800,000 children at risk for leukemia.[6]

More Treaties

Arms negotiations continued between the United States and the Soviet Union. In October 1986, Reagan met with the new Soviet premier, Mikhail Gorbachev, in Reykjavik, Iceland. Reagan and Gorbachev agreed to reduce the number of intermediate-range warheads. But the Soviet leader strongly objected to the Star Wars program. The Soviets still saw it as a military threat to their cities and territory.

Nevertheless, the two sides eventually agreed to reductions in intermediate-range weapons in Europe. On December 8, 1987, Reagan and Gorbachev signed the Intermediate-Range Nuclear Forces (INF) Treaty. The agreement eliminated all SS–20s, Pershing missiles, and cruise missiles from Europe— in all, 859 U.S. and 1,836 Soviet launch vehicles. It also required that the United States and the Soviet Union remove two thousand warheads from these missiles and return the warheads to their home countries.[7] For the first time, the Soviet Union agreed to on-site inspection of their military sites, so that the treaty could be verified. The United States Senate ratified the INF treaty on May 27, 1988.

More nuclear treaties followed in the 1990s, after the collapse of the Soviet Union. In 1991, the first Strategic Arms Reduction Treaty (START) limited each side to sixteen hundred "strategic delivery vehicles," meaning long-range bombers and intercontinental ballistic missiles (ICBMs), and six thousand long-range warheads. A START II treaty signed in 1993 cut the total of long-range weapons to three thousand in Russia and thirty-five hundred in the United States.[8] The Russian legislature finally ratified START II in April, 2000. Russia and the United States have also begun new negotiations, known as

START III, that would cut nuclear arsenals even further.

In 1996, most of the world's nuclear powers signed a new test ban treaty. This Comprehensive Test Ban Treaty (CTBT) forbids nuclear testing of all kinds, whether underground, in the atmosphere, or underwater. Two nuclear powers, India and Pakistan, have not signed the Comprehensive Test Ban Treaty. The nations that have signed—a total of 152 by July 1999—agree to abide by the treaty's terms, even if India and Pakistan do not. Although the United States has signed, the U.S. Senate has not yet ratified the CTBT. Senate leaders Jesse Helms and Trent Lott have blocked debate on the CTBT in order to have laws they favor passed. Many other legislators oppose this action. According to Joseph Biden, a senator from Delaware, "The unwillingness of Trent Lott to allow us to debate this treaty . . . is irresponsible, it is against the interests and wishes of the American people, it overrides the vast majority of the view of the United States senators, and it is stupid."[9]

Then, in October 1999, opponents of the Comprehensive Test Ban Treaty in the United States Senate called for a vote on the treaty—because they knew they had a majority who would vote against it. Indeed, the treaty was defeated by the Republican senators, who formed a majority in the Senate. A Senate majority can block international treaties signed by the president, and that happened in this case.[10]

The START talks and the Comprehensive Test Ban Treaty are important but small steps in lessening the danger of nuclear war. The world remains loaded with nuclear weapons. Russia has more than 20,000, while the United States has 12,000, France has 450, China has 400, and Britain has 260.[11] But both START and the Comprehensive Test Ban Treaty have been stopped by politics. Instead of supporting negotiations, politicians in many countries use them, or block them, to gain advantage for themselves and their political parties. This is an important reason for the slow progress of arms control, even as the spread of nuclear arms grows more dangerous.

5

Nuclear
Proliferation

Starting in 1989, the nations of the Warsaw Pact began throwing off their Communist governments. When Soviet allies such as Hungary and the Czech Republic left the Warsaw Pact, the military alliance led by the Soviets also ceased to exist. Within the Soviet Union, economic hard times and the loss of these European allies brought demand for a change. The Soviet government collapsed, and the Soviet Union broke up into fifteen independent nations.

The United States and its NATO allies won the Cold War. The conflict came to a peaceful conclusion. But both sides had

71

prepared themselves well. A gigantic arsenal of more than forty thousand nuclear weapons remained on what was once the territory of the Soviet Union. These weapons would still be targeted at the United States and at NATO countries in Europe in the event of war.

The Soviet arsenal included intercontinental ballistic missiles, tactical missiles, nuclear-tipped artillery shells, nuclear bombs, and radioactive land mines. Some of these weapons can be transported by an ordinary train or truck.

The old Soviet arsenal now belonged to the governments of Russia, Ukraine, Kazakhstan, and Belarus. A single nuclear superpower had turned into four new and independent nuclear powers. There were weaponmaking facilities all over the former Soviet Union. In addition, the former Soviet Union was home to thousands of engineers and scientists who knew how to build nuclear weapons. These people no longer worked for the Soviet government. They could offer their knowledge to any other country that wanted to hire them. They could bring nuclear weapons to the rest of the world.

After the Soviet breakup, some agreements were made to return nuclear weapons to Russia. In 1992, Ukraine agreed to give up several thousand tactical nuclear weapons that remained on its territory. The weapons were sent back to Russia. In the next year, Ukraine agreed to dismantle strategic nuclear weapons on its territory. But these actions do not mean that Ukrainian leaders have made peace with Russia, or even trust Russian leaders to respect

Ukraine's territory. An expert on Ukraine, Alexander
J. Motyl, has written,

> Unless the West provides the militarily impotent
> non-Russian states, especially Ukraine, with
> minimal security assurances, unless it allays their
> fears of being swallowed up by Russia, they will
> have no choice but to give priority to their
> immediate survival. . . . The very last message the
> West should convey to Ukrainians is, as one
> Western diplomat put it, "Give us your missiles
> and go to hell." With incentives like these,
> Ukraine may as well go to hell *with* its missiles.[1]

Fighting to Survive

Following the plan designed by Communist thinkers
in the nineteenth century, the Soviet government had
owned and controlled every business in the country.
The new Russian government of the 1990s did not
have the resources to operate these businesses. Many
people lost their jobs when the companies closed
down. The collapse of the Soviet Union caused economic chaos in Russia.

To make money, or just to survive, some former
Soviet scientists formed companies to sell nuclear
technology to foreign countries. To raise money, the
Russian military is selling Russian planes and missiles to foreign countries. Many of the weapons can
be used as nuclear delivery systems. Someday, the
Russian military may also sell old Soviet warheads.[2]

Many countries and organizations want these
nuclear weapons. Instead of building their own,
which can take years, they simply try to buy them.

One of the first such deals almost took place in 1991. A Soviet officer in eastern Germany offered to steal and sell a nuclear missile. He offered the missile to a member of Greenpeace, an international antinuclear organization, for $320,000. Greenpeace wanted to demonstrate a frightening fact: nuclear weapons were now available to anyone who had the money to buy them, anywhere in the world. At the last minute, however, the Soviet government withdrew the officer as well as the warhead from their base.[3]

The government of Russia sells nuclear technology in a busy world market. Russian manufacturers have sold Iran, North Korea, and Cuba breeder reactors, which produce bomb-grade plutonium. These reactors can produce enough nuclear fuel for several dozen bombs each year. Russia's customers can also buy nuclear bomb fuel, such as enriched uranium. This allows them to avoid the complicated process of enriching uranium in a laboratory. A leader of Russia's space program, Vladimir Lobachev, once said, "There are no secrets. We will sell anything, in any form, which will make a profit."[4]

Prestige and Proliferation

Nuclear proliferation has become a growing problem. At one time, only the superpowers had these weapons. Now, China, Great Britain, France, Israel, India, and Pakistan have joined the nuclear ranks. Other countries, including Iraq, have nuclear programs but do not yet have the weapons ready. More

Dr. J. Robert Oppenheimer, as scientific director of the Manhattan Project, coordinated the design and building of the world's first nuclear weapons. Later, Oppenheimer was appalled at the power he had unleashed—the potential for destruction through nuclear proliferation.

than twenty countries have ballistic missiles that can carry nuclear warheads.

Countries that cannot afford nuclear weapons can build arsenals of chemical and biological weapons. Or they can build radiological bombs. These are weapons that use conventional explosives to disperse large amounts of radioactive isotopes, such as cesium–137 and strontium–90. In large enough doses, these isotopes harm victims through radiation poisoning, which damages or destroys the cells that make up the body's skin, tissue, and organs.

The world's future nuclear powers may include Iran, Libya, Syria, Turkey, Algeria, and Taiwan. Even Japan—the only country in the world to suffer a nuclear attack—is prepared to begin new weapons programs. The country's constitution, written after World War II, makes offensive military action by Japan illegal. But Japanese leaders worry over political conflict between Communist China and Taiwan, and between North and South Korea. In August 1998, North Korea test-fired a missile over Japanese territory. In March 1999, Japanese ships fired warning shots at North Korean ships. Three months later, South Korea sank a North Korean patrol boat. Fearing another war in East Asia, Japan now seeks to develop a missile-defense system with the help of the United States.[5]

Many countries that are developing weapons claim they need them to defend against stronger enemies. Others simply invest in nuclear weapons as a matter of pride. They see nuclear weapons as placing them among the world's most powerful nations. They also want to offer their know-how to other countries. Knowledge and training in nuclear weapons can be sold as easily as any other export.

The end of the Cold War made the world more uncertain. Few governments can be sure of who their friends are. In particular, they cannot be sure of the United States. They know that the United States supported Iraq during the 1980s. It supplied Iraq with many of its weapons and looked away when Iraq started a nuclear program. Now, the United States considers Iraq and its leader, Saddam Hussein, one of its worst enemies. With nuclear weapons, the smaller countries of the world no longer have to depend on other countries to defend them the way South Korea, a non-nuclear nation, still depends on the United States.

Proliferation and Big Business

Business also helps the proliferation of nuclear weapons. Many private companies manufacture military weapons. Some of these companies also sell machinery that can be used to build nuclear weapons. These companies will sell their goods to any country willing to buy. Many business owners do not feel bound by international laws and treaties signed by governments. Instead, these agreements represent obstacles to be overcome, like customs duties and taxes.

For the sake of doing business, several foreign countries have been helping Libya's leader, General Mu'ammar Gaddafi, build missiles and develop chemical weapons. According to writer Mansour O. El-Kikhia,

> With technology provided by the German firm Imhausen, research and development of biological weapons are currently being undertaken in the little known town of Taminhint, northwest of the city of Sabha in south-central Libya. . . .
>
> China and North Korea have also been actively assisting Libya's missile development. The Chinese, in particular, have received a first installment of two billion American dollars [from Libya] . . . to coproduce with Libya an accurate missile capable of striking targets over 1,500 kilometers in range.[6]

Some companies and nations claim to sell goods only for peaceful purposes. In fact, many of these goods are known as dual-use. They can be used for peaceful or military purposes. For many countries, dual-use technology has become a key method of building a nuclear arsenal. They buy special furnaces for casting bomb casings or photographic equipment for use in weapons testing. They buy industrial lasers for machining bomb parts. They buy "heavy water," which is used to control chain reactions inside nuclear plants. Many of the companies that make the sales do not ask, and do not care, how the goods will be used.

Dual-use goods also include computers, rocket engines, ordinary explosives, chemicals, and complex machinery. Some German companies sell dual-use chemicals, which they label as pesticides, to the North African country of Libya. These chemicals can indeed be used as pesticides. They also can be used to make chemical weapons.

The Hanford Engineer Works plant in Richland, Washington, produced plutonium for use in the Fat Man bomb at the end of World War II. Once the only site capable of producing plutonium, it is now just one plant among many such facilities around the world.

In the 1980s, Libya also manufactured poison gas at a plant known as Rabta. The gas was placed in rockets, bombs, and artillery shells. The work was carried out with the help of private companies from Germany and Japan.

When a newspaper report revealed that German companies were supplying chemical weapons to

Libya, a scandal took place in Germany. In response, Gaddafi announced that he did not intend to make poison gas. Soon thereafter, in March 1990, a large fire broke out at Rabta. A *Time* magazine report said,

> In 1990 [Gaddafi] shut down the Rabta plant after Washington threatened to attack it with warplanes and publicly identified European companies that had provided equipment. But U.S. satellites soon discovered that Rabta's equipment had been moved and stored in underground bunkers a mile away.[7]

In the United States, the government often fights within itself over dual-use exports. In general, the Department of Commerce supports this trade because it wants to promote businesses in the United States. The Department of Defense often opposes the sale of dual-use technology for the sake of military security. The Department of State often makes the final decision. It first considers whether the goods are being sold to an ally or to an enemy of the United States. Because the State Department wants to help those countries it considers friendly, allies find it much easier to get dangerous weapons. The United States has helped private weapons sales to Iran, Pakistan, and Iraq. At the time, it saw these countries as U.S. allies. By the late 1990s, in all three cases, the government had changed its mind.

Israel

One nation that has long been allied with the United States is Israel. The United States and other countries have been helping Israel create nuclear weapons for more than forty years. United States officials still see Israel as an important friend in a very dangerous and important region: the Middle East.

The leaders of Israel believe they must have nuclear weapons to defend themselves. Israel is a tiny country, about as big as Massachusetts. To the southeast is Egypt, against whom Israel has fought several wars. Syria, another old enemy, lies to the north; and to the east is Iraq, a powerful country that has vowed to drive the people of Israel into the Mediterranean Sea.

Immediately after it was founded in 1948, Israel had to fight a war with its foreign enemies. In the 1950s, Israel bought a nuclear research reactor from France. Construction of the reactor began in 1958 at Dimona, in Israel's Negev Desert. The reactor processed enriched uranium and plutonium. The reactor at Dimona allowed Israel to build a small arsenal of nuclear missiles, which Israeli leaders named Jerichos.

In 1967, a war broke out between Israel and Egypt. Just before the fighting began, Israel prepared its first two nuclear bombs. In 1973, during the Yom Kippur War, Israel again readied its Jericho missiles. Israel's military leaders planned to use the missiles if their enemies began overrunning the country. But Israel won the war without using its nuclear weapons.

Israel again readied a nuclear attack in 1991. Its old enemy, Iraq, fired thirty-nine long-range Scud missiles at Israel, hitting the cities of Tel Aviv and Haifa. The Scud warheads were armed with high explosives. They also could have been carrying chemical weapons. After the Scud attacks began, Israel went on a nuclear alert. The Israelis were prepared to launch nuclear missiles in case Iraq loaded its missiles with poison gas.[8]

Israel has stockpiled more than two hundred nuclear bombs at the Dimona plant. The newest ballistic missiles in this arsenal have a range of five thousand miles. They can fly far enough to hit any point in Europe, the Middle East, or North Africa. Israel has also armed itself with nuclear-capable aircraft and submarines. If Israel's enemies ever succeed in destroying its aircraft and missiles, the submarines can still make a nuclear strike from underneath the sea.

Israel built many of its modern weapons during the 1980s. Israel has not signed the Non-proliferation Treaty. The United States considers Israel, as well as all of its allies in NATO, exempt from anti-proliferation laws passed by the U.S. Congress.

Iraq

Iraq's drive for the nuclear bomb began in the late 1970s, after Saddam Hussein became president. In 1976, Iraq bought a nuclear research reactor named *Osirak* from France, the country that had sold the Dimona reactor to Israel. As a condition of the contract, France insisted that Iraq sign the Non-proliferation Treaty, and Hussein agreed.

Hussein wanted Iraq to be the first Arab country to possess a nuclear bomb. He wanted to make Iraq as powerful as Israel, which was the only country in the Middle East to own nuclear weapons. The Iraqi reactor program moved ahead smoothly in the late 1970s. It was so successful that Israel began to see it as a grave threat. On June 7, 1981, Israel destroyed *Osirak* in a bombing raid.

Iraq pressed ahead, intending to rebuild its nuclear program from the ground up. Iraq set up companies to import the necessary machinery: precision tools, explosives designed for use in a nuclear bomb, parts for cyclotrons, and guidance systems for ballistic missiles. Some of the information and materials came from companies—German, British, French, and American—willing to supply it. Iraq got some information by using stolen documents or by surfing the Internet. Iraqi scientists built some of the equipment on their own.

Then, in the summer of 1990, Saddam Hussein ordered the invasion of Kuwait. During the Gulf War that followed in 1991, many of Iraq's nuclear facilities were destroyed in bombing raids. More nuclear material was destroyed by UN inspectors after the war.

In late 1998, Iraq put a halt to all UN inspections on its territory. By this time, Saddam Hussein had restored much of his country's nuclear industry. His government still has the plans and many of the parts needed to build nuclear weapons. By 1999, Iraq lacked only nuclear warheads. As soon as it gets the warheads, either by building them or buying them from another country, it will become the second nuclear power in the Middle East.

Pakistan and India

In 1974, India carried out its first test of a nuclear weapon. The explosion took place in the desert of Rajasthan, near India's border with Pakistan, its neighbor to the west. That first test began a nuclear rivalry that has brought the two countries to the brink of mutual destruction several times.

India and Pakistan have been rivals since 1948, when Pakistan was created from parts of northern India. Pakistan's population is mostly Islamic, while a majority of India's people are Hindu. The two countries have fought several conventional wars along their long frontier.

In 1972, Pakistan's president Zulfikar Ali Bhutto ordered scientists in his country to begin a nuclear weapons program. Bhutto sought the renown that would come with building the first nuclear bomb in an Islamic country. He also wanted to match India's nuclear program. Pakistan rushed ahead with its own nuclear project after India tested its first nuclear weapon in 1974.

Pakistan's nuclear program had help from several other countries. The most important aid came from Communist China, which provided equipment and training for Pakistani scientists. China also allowed Pakistan to copy the design of its own nuclear missiles. China had a good reason for helping: The Chinese saw Pakistan as a useful ally against their mutual rival, India.

In the 1980s, Pakistan also received cooperation from the United States. At this time, the Soviet

Union had invaded Pakistan's neighbor, Afghanistan. In the interest of fighting the Soviet occupation of Afghanistan, the United States gave Pakistan money as well as military technology. Despite the fact that the United States had pledged to stop nuclear proliferation, U.S. officials raised no objections to Pakistan's nuclear program.

Pakistan did not have as much money to spend on nuclear weapons as the world's other nuclear powers. But Pakistan did have nuclear power plants. In the 1970s, Pakistani scientists learned how to reprocess plutonium. They used plutonium from nuclear power plants and turned it into bomb-grade plutonium. Using plutonium in this way is much less expensive than enriching uranium.

By the end of the 1980s, Pakistan had successfully built a nuclear weapon. Through the 1980s, Pakistan built a small nuclear arsenal. In May 1989, India responded by testing its first ballistic missile, the Agni. The missile can deliver the country's nuclear weapons to Pakistan or as far away as Beijing, the capital of its old enemy, Communist China.

In the meantime, the conflict between India and Pakistan worsened. The two countries both claimed to own Kashmir. This province lies high in the Himalaya Mountains, on Pakistan's northeastern border. Many of the people of Kashmir are Islamic and want independence from India. Pakistan wants to make Kashmir a part of its territory, but the government of India does not want to give it up. A guerrilla movement targeted Indian police and soldiers, as well as Hindu civilians. In August 1999, a *New York Times* journalist described the situation:

> At first, the insurgency was home-grown. Kashmiri youth, shouting *azadi*, or freedom, became guerrillas, trying to send India packing with a few well-placed bombs and high-profile kidnappings. . . . To New Delhi, this was a threat to its nation-hood, to Islamabad [the capital of Pakistan] an opportunity to wage war by proxy. India has since tried to stamp out the revolt with all the fury of an enraged elephant, while Pakistan has tried to provoke the uprising further and arm it and bend it to its will.[9]

The conflict between India and Pakistan may result in another war, which could very easily go nuclear. The danger is increased by the political instability of both nations. In the years since World War II, several of India's leaders and political candidates have been assassinated. Pakistan has undergone coups as well as violence between opposing political factions. The lack of stability makes it hard to predict the willingness of a future leader to use nuclear weapons.

In October 1999, the Pakistani government of Prime Minister Nawaz Sharif was overthrown by military forces under the leadership of General Pervez Musharraf. Government ministers were fired, the Pakistani parliament dissolved, and martial law was declared. Musharraf's coup was wildly popular among Pakistanis who believed that Sharif did not stand up to India in the conflict over Kashmir.[10]

More Proliferation

Dangerous weapons systems have spread to several other countries. Although it is a very poor nation, North Korea has manufactured missiles capable of carrying nuclear weapons. This greatly worries the United States as well as North Korea's neighbors, Japan and South Korea. In 1994, the United States agreed to help North Korea develop peaceful nuclear energy, in exchange for a freeze on North Korea's nuclear weapons program. The freeze did not last. In August 1998, North Korea tested one of its missiles by firing it over the ocean in Japanese territory. In the summer of 1999, it threatened to test another missile, one that could reach the United States.

North Korea uses these tests, and the threats of more tests, to get what it desperately needs: imports of food, money, and energy. Several countries donated these items to North Korea, but the United States has instituted a trade embargo, meaning it bans United States companies from selling their goods there. North Korea wants the trade embargo lifted. According to an article in the *Sarasota Herald-Tribune*:

> The leaders in Pyongyang [the North Korean capital] don't seem to want either to give up the weapons of mass destruction that they can use for blackmail, or to accept a broader relationship with the outside world that could weaken their own hold on power inside North Korea.[11]

Another conflict in Korea may involve nuclear weapons, used by either North Korea or by the

Observers are silhouetted against the immense cloud of smoke and dust created by the testing of a nuclear weapon. Many companies in the business of making military weapons want to make a profit and downplay the potential destructiveness of nuclear weapons.

United States, which pledges to defend South Korea in case of attack.

When new conflicts break out, nuclear weapons may spread to countries that did not have them before. In the spring of 1999, a war began in Serbia, a republic in the European country of Yugoslavia. NATO, led by the United States, began bombing Serbia, which had no nuclear arsenal of its own. But Serbia is an old ally of Russia, which has thousands of nuclear weapons. In the future, to help Serbia, Russia may sell or simply give some nuclear weapons to the Serbian government. This is an important reason to solve conflicts over territory or resources before they turn into wars.

A few other nations have built nuclear weapons and then given them up. One of these nations is South Africa. During the 1980s, Israel gave South Africa the materials and training necessary to build nuclear devices. The government of South Africa wanted a nuclear arsenal to use in a possible civil war. At the time, South Africa was sharply divided between white and black citizens. A system of laws known as "apartheid" created separate neighborhoods, schools, and public facilities for blacks and whites.

In the 1990s, this policy of separation ended. The laws of apartheid were struck down, and whites and blacks now mix more freely in South Africa. The country has also put a stop to its nuclear program.

Several countries in Latin America could easily build or buy nuclear weapons. But Brazil, Argentina, and Chile have decided to hold to the 1967 treaty that bans nuclear weapons from Latin America. As a result, South America remains a nuclear-free zone.

Other regions, like Antarctica and Scandinavia, have remained nuclear-free through a combination of treaties and self-determination. But to stop proliferation, many more countries must follow their example. They will not do so unless they see nuclear arsenals as useless—or as too expensive, troublesome, and dangerous to keep.

6

The Future

There are many different ways for a nuclear war to start. Some possibilities include:

- A conflict over territory may begin between two rival states, such as India and Pakistan. The leaders of Pakistan realize that India's army is much larger. To win the war quickly, they may decide to attack immediately with a nuclear weapon. They may see this weapon as their only chance to win.

- A terrorist group may buy a small nuclear weapon from a Russian commander. The group will use the weapon for blackmail. If their demands for money, or something else, are not met, they will set off the bomb.

- A civil war may begin inside a country with nuclear arms. One side may take control of a tactical nuclear missile. No complex computer codes or key systems are needed to launch the missile. It can simply be fired like ordinary artillery.

- Through a human or computer error, a country with nuclear arms that is conducting a test may accidentally fire a nuclear missile at its neighbor. Officers at an air force headquarters may accidentally instruct one of their pilots to drop a nuclear bomb on another country.

- A computer "hacker" may try to break into a military computer system. In the United States or some other country, the hacker may try to obtain launch codes and electronically instruct a nuclear missile to fire. Or the hacker may cause computerized radar systems to warn of an impending attack from a foreign country. The time to react may be much shorter than the time needed to make sure the message is false, so a launch could be ordered even though there would be no threat.

The more countries that obtain weapons of mass destruction, the more possibilities there are for a nuclear war. Weapons of mass destruction have not ended war, nor have they ended conflicts over territory, over minerals, or over control of vital resources such as oil and water.

Deterrence in the Future

Some people argue that nuclear weapons have made the world safer. Instead of causing wars, nuclear weapons help to deter them. They encourage countries to settle their conflicts peacefully. The idea of deterrence depends on the belief that nobody wants to fight a nuclear war because it would probably mean the destruction of their own country. It might even mean the end of the world, or a "nuclear winter," in which all life on earth is destroyed by radiation and by the environmental effects caused by immense nuclear explosions.

Those who believe in deterrence point out that nuclear weapons have not been used in wartime since World War II. For the forty-five years since, the United States and the Soviet Union have never fought each other directly. The superpowers have enough nuclear weapons to destroy each other many times. But both sides have kept very close watch on nuclear weapons. They do not allow their allies to control their bombs and missiles. Soviet officers commanded the missile batteries in Cuba in 1962. U.S. officers held the nuclear keys and codes in Western Europe.

Leaders of both sides understood that they could never actually use nuclear weapons. In fact, they realized nuclear weapons were useful only as a threat. Otherwise, they were useless.

Closing the Nuclear Ranks

Other people disagree with deterrence. They see deterrence as the wrong idea, or an idea that no

Activists from the Forum Against Nuclear Testing (FANT) protest the five nuclear tests conducted by India on May 16, 1998. Though only five seconds long, those tests shifted the balance of nuclear power in a very troubled area.

longer works. The United States has helped other nations buy or build nuclear weapons. Russia sells nuclear technology to willing buyers. Scientists from the former Soviet Union sell their knowledge. European countries sell machinery, computers, and other goods that can be used to build nuclear weapons.

Soon, the nuclear ranks will grow even larger. They will include many small and nonaligned nations. These nations will have small arsenals, with only a few nuclear weapons or even a single one. The threat of a worldwide nuclear war will not deter them. Instead, they will see nuclear weapons as their most useful tool on the battlefield. Such weapons make them just as strong as more powerful enemies who possess larger armies and more ships, planes, and tanks.

One thing is certain: Nuclear weapons have not prevented conventional wars over territory or conflicts between rival ethnic groups. If a war breaks out again between Israel and the Arab states, Israel will be ready to respond to a chemical attack with a Jericho missile. If fighting breaks out along the border between India and Pakistan, India will target the Pakistani nuclear reactor at Kahuta. Pakistan may try to drop nuclear bombs on the crowded Indian cities.

What can be done to stop the spread of weapons of mass destruction? What can be done to prevent their use? One possibility is to place responsibility for control of nuclear weapons in the hands of the United Nations. To do this, the UN would have to keep track of all nuclear weapons. It must keep careful records of where the weapons are made. It must also find out where they are stored. It must keep track of the materials used for nuclear weapons, including uranium and plutonium.

Then the UN must strictly enforce treaties limiting or banning nuclear weapons. Its members must agree to a ban on all testing. They must agree to stop producing nuclear weapons and to stop inventing new ones.

Even so, many nations still believe they have the right to own nuclear weapons. The world will have to try a different kind of deterrence. This deterrence is economic, not military. Nuclear weapons must become too expensive.

To make nuclear weapons too expensive, the United Nations must make sure that weapons treaties are followed. If a country breaks the agreement, the member countries of the UN must agree to punish it. The violating country must not be allowed to trade with other countries. If it cannot sell its goods to other countries, or buy goods from other countries, that nation will grow poorer. Eventually, its people, government, and military will suffer. The ban on trade must continue until the country's leaders agree to stop breaking international law.

If this punishment does not work, military force must be used. The members of the United Nations must all take part. They will have to remove the nuclear weapons by force.

One final step remains. This was the step first suggested by businessman Bernard Baruch in his Baruch Plan just after World War II. Nations that already have nuclear weapons must agree to destroy all of them.

Preparing for the Future

These ideas may not work. The countries of the UN rarely agree on a common policy. In addition, the UN has not been successful in disarming dangerous countries such as Iraq. In the 1990s, Iraq defied

UN sanctions on its weapons program. It stopped UN inspectors from visiting its weapons factories. This action brought on the bombing of Iraq's territory. But Iraqi leaders are willing to have their country bombed for the sake of continuing their weapons program.

In the future, the United States may fight a nuclear war. In World War II, it was the only country armed with nuclear weapons. The next time, it will not be. The war may be fought in a foreign country, thousands of miles away. Or it may be fought in the United States itself.

The United States has prepared itself for nuclear weapons and chemical warfare. The U.S. Congress passed the Defense Against Weapons of Mass Destruction Act in 1996. The government will spend money to train first responders—police, fire fighters, and medical emergency teams—in 120 of the nation's largest cities. The program is already running but is scheduled for completion in 2001. It will also allow each city to buy detection, decontamination, and protective equipment.

Albert Einstein, who was one of the first scientists to reveal the secret power of the atom, thought there might be one other way to prepare. Perhaps scientists could persuade the most powerful countries of the world to cooperate, rather than compete. In a letter, he described how it would work:

> There are in the principal countries scientists who are really influential and who know how to get a hearing with political leaders. . . . The idea is that these men should bring combined pressure on the

political leaders in their countries in order to bring about an internationalization of military power . . . this radical step . . . seems the only alternative to a secret technical arms race.[1]

In other words, the world should create an international military force that would share all of its technology and nuclear secrets. Einstein feared his idea would prove impossible. But he saw no other way. If the arms race is not stopped, one day the world will step over the brink and engage in nuclear warfare. Such a war may spread, as many other wars have. The earth's environment may be damaged. Like the dinosaurs, human beings could face extinction. Unlike the dinosaurs, humans will have brought extinction upon themselves.

Chapter Notes

Chapter 1. A Cloud Over the World

1. Robert B. Asprey, *The German High Command at War: Hindenburg & Ludendorff Conduct World War I* (New York: William Morrow and Company, Inc., 1991), p. 383.

2. Bela Silard and William Lanouette, *Genius in the Shadows: A Biography of Leo Szilard, the Man Behind the Bomb* (New York: Charles Scribner's Sons, 1992), pp. 198–202.

3. Ronald W. Clark, *Einstein: The Life and Times* (New York: The World Publishing Company, 1971), p. 556.

4. Richard Rhodes, *Dark Sun: The Making of the Hydrogen Bomb* (New York: Simon and Schuster, 1995), p. 131.

5. Benjamin King and Timothy Kutta, *Impact: The History of Germany's V-Weapons in World War II* (Rockville Center, N.Y.: Sarpedon, 1998), pp. 313–329.

6. Philip Nobile, ed., *Judgment at the Smithsonian* (New York: Marlowe & Company, n.d.), pp. 26–27.

7. Ibid., p. 43.

8. Godfrey Hodgson, *The Colonel: The Life and Wars of Henry Stimson, 1867–1950* (New York: Alfred A. Knopf, Inc., 1990), pp. 323–324.

9. David McCullough, *Truman* (New York: Simon and Schuster, 1992), p. 395.

10. Robert H. Ferrell, *Off the Record: The Private Papers of Harry S. Truman* (New York: Harper & Row, 1980), pp. 55–56.

11. Gar Alperovitz, *The Decision to Use the Atomic Bomb* (New York: Vintage Books, 1996), p. 187.

12. Rhodes, p. 175.

13. Alperovitz, p. 544.

14. John Hersey, *Hiroshima* (New York: Alfred A. Knopf, 1985), p. 25.

15. Nobile, p. 101.

16. Ibid., pp. 128–129.

17. Takashi Nagai, *The Bells of Nagasaki* (Tokyo: Kodansha International, 1984), p. 29.

Chapter 2. The Cold War

1. David McCullough, *Truman* (New York: Simon and Schuster, 1992), p. 458.

2. Gar Alperovitz, *The Decision to Use the Atomic Bomb* (New York: Vintage Books, 1996), p. 4.

3. Godfrey Hodgson, *The Colonel: The Life and Wars of Henry Stimson, 1867–1950* (New York: Alfred A. Knopf, Inc., 1990), p. 331.

4. James Grant, *Bernard Baruch: The Adventures of a Wall Street Legend* (New York: Simon and Schuster, 1983), p. 311.

5. Richard Rhodes, *Dark Sun: The Making of the Hydrogen Bomb* (New York: Simon and Schuster, 1995), pp. 241–242.

6. Jonathan Weisgall, *Operation Crossroads: The Atomic Tests at Bikini Atoll* (Annapolis, Md.: Naval Institute Press, 1994), p. 194.

7. Rhodes, p. 262.

8. James Roland, "Inching Toward Armageddon," *Sarasota Herald-Tribune*, August 15, 1999, p. 6E.

9. Rhodes, pp. 294–295.

10. Ibid., p. 343.

11. Ibid., pp. 165–175.

Chapter 3. The Atomic Age

1. Richard Rhodes, *Dark Sun: The Making of the*

Hydrogen Bomb (New York: Simon and Schuster, 1995), pp. 444–453.

2. Jim Mann, "North Korea May Explode Next," reprinted in *Sarasota Herald-Tribune*, July 24, 1999, p. 17A.

3. Carl B. Feldbaum and Ronald J. Bee, *Looking the Tiger in the Eye: Confronting the Nuclear Threat* (New York: Harper & Row, 1988), p. 136.

4. Ibid.

5. Aleksandr Fursenko and Timothy Naftal, *"One Hell of a Gamble": Khruschev, Castro and Kennedy, 1958–1964* (New York: W. W. Norton and Company, 1997), pp. 216–225.

6. Elie Abel, *The Missiles of October: The Story of the Cuban Missile Crisis, 1962* (London: MacGibbon & Kee Ltd., 1966), p. 125.

7. Theodore C. Sorensen, *Kennedy* (New York: Harper & Row, 1965) , p. 519.

8. Philip Nobile, ed., *Judgment at the Smithsonian* (New York: Marlowe & Company, n.d.), pp. 113–115.

9. Ira Helfand, "Effects of a Nuclear Explosion," Physicians for Social Responsibility Web site, n.d., <www.psr.org/Helfand1.htm> (August 15, 1999).

10. David Rush, M.D., and Jack Geiger, M.D., "The National Cancer Institute Report on Radioactive Iodine Fallout from Nuclear Weapons Testing: Preliminary Critique," n.d., <www.psrus.org/rush.htm> (August 15, 1999).

11. "Nuclear Q & A," Bulletin of the Atomic Scientists Web site, n.d., <www.bullatomsci.org> (August 15, 1999).

12. Michael D'Antonio, *Atomic Harvest: Hanford and the Lethal Toll of America's Nuclear Arsenal* (New York: Crown Publishers, 1993), p. 286.

13. "The Plutonium Threat," Nuclear Control Institute Web site, n.d., <www.nci.org> (August 15, 1999).

Chapter 4. Making Treaties

1. Robert Cole, *A Traveller's History of France* (New York: Interlink Books, 1997), p. 178.

2. Patrick Glynn, *Closing Pandora's Box: Arms Races, Arms Control, and the History of the Cold War* (New York: Basic Books, 1987), p. 270; Dan Caldwell, "From SALT to START: Limiting Strategic Nuclear Weapons," in *Encyclopedia of Arms Control and Disarmament* (New York: Charles Scribner's Sons, 1993), Vol. II, p. 900.

3. Glynn, p. 308.

4. Janne E. Nolan, "The INF Treaty: Eliminating Intermediate Range Nuclear Missiles, 1987 to the Present," *Encyclopedia of Arms Control and Disarmament*, (New York: Charles Scribner's Sons, 1993), Vol. II. p. 957.

5. Ronald Reagan, *An American Life* (New York: Simon and Schuster, 1990), pp. 574–575.

6. Helen Broinowski Caldicott, *A Desperate Passion: An Autobiography* (New York: W. W. Norton & Co., 1996), pp. 313–314.

7. Nolan, p. 959.

8. Caldwell, p. 911.

9. Geneva Oberholser, "Bring Test Ban Treaty to a Vote," reprinted in *Sarasota Herald-Tribune*, July 23, 1999, p.11A.

10. John Cloud, "Is It Trick or Treaty?" *Time*, October 25, 1999, p. 52.

11. "Nuclear Q & A," Bulletin of the Atomic Scientists Web site, n.d., <www.bullatomsci.org> (August 15, 1999).

Chapter 5. Nuclear Proliferation

1. Alexander J. Motyl, *Dilemmas of Independence: Ukraine After Totalitarianism* (New York: Council on Foreign Relations, Inc., 1993), pp. 187–188.

2. William E. Burrows and Robert Windrem, *Critical Mass: The Dangerous Race for Superweapons*

in a Fragmenting World (New York: Simon and Schuster, 1994), pp. 116–117.

3. Ibid., pp. 246–251.

4. Ibid., p. 264.

5. Associated Press, "Report Reflects Japan's Anxiety over Asia," *Sarasota Herald Tribune*, July 28, 1999, p. 7A.

6. Mansour O. El-Kikhia, *Libya's Qaddafi: The Politics of Contradiction* (Gainesville, Fla.: University Press of Florida, 1997), p. 95.

7. Douglas Waller, "Target Gaddafi, Again," *Time*, April 1, 1996, pp. 46–47.

8. Burrows and Windrem, pp. 279–280.

9. Barry Bearak, "Kashmir a Crushed Jewel Caught in a Vise of Hatred," *The New York Times*, August 12, 1999, p. 1A.

10. Romesh Rathesar, "The Good News Coup?" *Time*, October 25, 1999, pp. 56–57.

11. Jim Mann, "North Korea May Explode Next," *Sarasota Herald-Tribune*, July 24, 1999, p. 17A.

Chapter 6. The Future

1. Ronald W. Clark, *Einstein: The Life and Times* (New York: The World Publishing Company, 1971), pp. 575–576.

Glossary

ABMs (anti-ballistic missiles)—Defensive missiles designed to destroy ICBMs (see below) in flight.

atomic bomb—A bomb whose explosive force comes from energy stored inside the atom.

ballistic missile—A missile that is launched into the atmosphere and returns to earth under the force of gravity.

Cold War—A global political conflict between the United States and the Soviet Union, lasting from the end of World War II until the collapse of the Soviet Union in the early 1990s.

conventional weapons—Non-nuclear weapons such as armored tanks and infantry.

cruise missile—Shorter-range, ground-launched missiles designed in the 1980s for use in Europe.

détente—The general easing of relations between the two superpowers, the United States and the Soviet Union, beginning in the 1970s.

dual-use—Technology or materials that can be used for military or for peaceful purposes.

fission—The act of splitting atomic nuclei, which in turn can release explosive force.

fusion—The act of combining atomic nuclei, which in turn creates new elements and can give off an explosive force.

hydrogen bomb—A weapon developed in the 1950s that derives its force from the fusion of isotopes (see below) of the element hydrogen.

ICBM (intercontinental ballistic missile)—A weapon designed to be launched from the territory of the United States, or from that of the Soviet Union, and reach the territory of the other nation by flying across the Arctic.

isotope—Different kinds of atoms of the same element. For example, U–235 and U–238 are different types of uranium.

MAD (mutual assured destruction)—A doctrine designed to prevent nuclear war by threatening an immediate nuclear reprisal and the annihilation of the attacking country.

megaton—A measure of explosive force of a nuclear weapon. One megaton equals the force of one million tons of TNT explosive.

MIRVs (Multiple Independently Targetable Reentry Vehicles)—Ballistic missiles that have several warheads designed to separate from the missile itself in mid-flight and then fly to different targets.

NATO (North Atlantic Treaty Organization)—A military alliance of North American and European nations, originally formed to protect Western Europe from a Soviet attack.

neutron—A particle present in the nucleus of an atom.

plutonium—An artificial element that can be used to fuel nuclear reactors as well as nuclear weapons.

proliferation—The spread of nuclear weapons to countries and groups that previously did not possess them.

radioactivity—A property of certain elements in which changes in the nucleus (center) of the atom cause it to emit energy. In large enough doses, radioactivity is harmful to humans, animals, plants, and the environment.

radiological bombs—Weapons designed to explode and spread poisonous radioactive isotopes rather than to destroy by blast and heat.

ratify—To pass into law.

uranium—A radioactive element that, in certain forms, can be used to fuel powerfully destructive weapons.

Warsaw Pact—An alliance of Eastern European nations under the leadership of the Soviet Union, formed to balance the NATO alliance in Europe.

Further Reading

Bernstein, Jeremy. *Albert Einstein and the Frontiers of Physics*. New York: Oxford University Press, 1996.

Cross, Robin. *Technology of War*. Austin, Texas: Raintree Steck-Vaughn Publishers, 1994.

Epler, Doris. *The Berlin Wall: How It Rose and Why It Fell*. Brookfield, Conn.: Millbrook Press, Inc., 1992.

Grant, R. G. *Hiroshima and Nagasaki* (New Perspectives series). Austin, Texas: Raintree Steck-Vaughn Publishers, 1998.

Hakim, Joy. *War, Peace, and All That Jazz*. New York: Oxford University Press, 1995.

Hersey, John. *Hiroshima*. New York: Alfred A. Knopf, 1985.

Martin, Laurence. *Nuclear Warfare* (Modern Military Techniques series). Minneapolis: Lerner Publications, 1989.

Pasachoff, Naomi. *Marie Curie and the Science of Radioactivity*. New York: Oxford University Press, 1996.

Stein, R. Conrad. *The Manhattan Project* (Cornerstones of Freedom series). Chicago: Children's Press, 1993.

Internet Addresses

Bulletin of the Atomic Scientists

<www.bullatomsci.org>

This is the Web site of *The Bulletin of the Atomic Scientists*, a magazine that measures the risk of a nuclear war by the Doomsday Clock. A variety of articles is available online, as is an extensive reference section on nuclear arsenals, testing, and treaties.

Nukefix

<www.nukefix.org>

A site that allows the user to calculate the risks of nuclear conflict. Among other tools, the program helps users understand and analyze policies of deterrence and the effects of current weapons treaties.

Physicians for Social Responsibility

<www.psr.org>

A site maintained by an organization of doctors concerned with social and political issues, among them nuclear weapons and nuclear energy.

The Center for Defense Information

<www.cdi.org>

A nonprofit research organization that monitors military affairs, current weapons systems, and the world's ongoing political conflicts.

The Nuclear Age Peace Foundation

<www.wagingpeace.org>

A site whose writers advocate complete nuclear abolition and disarmament, offering information, activism, and contests encouraging user participation and input.

The Nuclear Control Institute

<www.nci.org>

A site focusing on environmental and health risks of nuclear energy and nuclear weapons manufacturing.

Index